Door County's Best Hikes and Outdoor Adventures

77 Hikes and Outdoor Adventures in the Best Natural Places in Door County, Wisconsin

Joe and Janet Mrazek

Photo Credits

Janet Mrazek
Martha Scully Beller

⚜ Old Homestead Press
oldhomesteadpress@gmail.com

TABLE OF CONTENTS

5

GUIDE TO ICONS

 beach

 cross-country skiing

 fishing

 lighthouse

 restrooms

 snowshoeing

 wildflowers

 biking

 dogs allowed

 hiking

 paddling

 scenic overlook

 walking

 wildlife

DOOR COUNTY MAP

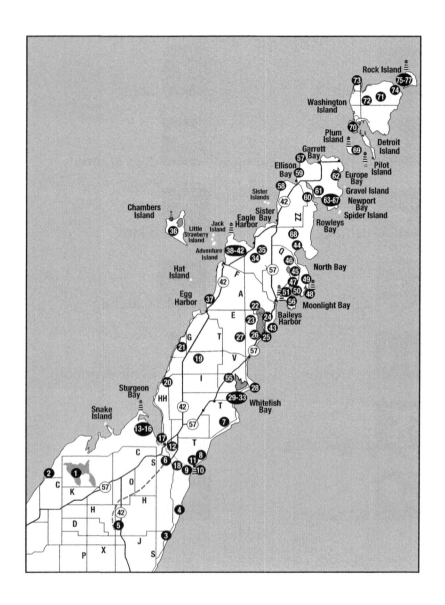

INTRODUCTION

Door County has its obvious charms—the quaint villages, the boats plying the waters just offshore, the brilliant fall foliage, and the cool summer days—these are the things about this place that keeps millions of visitors coming back year after year.

For us it is a subtler draw. We can think of few better pleasures than walking the trails along the shores of the Mink River Estuary in mid-May surrounded by migratory birds, tossing on a pair of snowshoes on a bluebird day in February, and blazing trails through the local nature preserve, or that perfect fall day enveloped in brilliant colors. We'll even take a blustery winter day with a stiff wind off Lake Michigan.

Roaming and rambling around Door County has been a life-long pursuit, and we thought the best way to capture that spirit was by sharing some of our favorite places with others. Most of these spots we found on our own, back before Google maps and even the Internet, when word of mouth and traipsing down many dead-end roads were how you found places to hike. Other places are new, recently protected by local land trusts or towns and opened up to the public in recent years. Some spots we read about in magazines and even, yes, on the internet. Sure, it is easier now and secret places don't stay secret for long, but we hope you will share our wanderlust and sense of discovery hiking these trails for the first time. Door County is an amazing place to discover the outdoors, whether you have considerable hiking, paddling, or mountain biking experience, or you just want to take a casual walk and enjoy a pretty view.

This book covers our absolute favorite places to get outside for a walk or a hike in Door County. Some areas are incredibly popular. Others see little visitation. We hope you'll treat them with the reverence they deserve. In the interest of preserving Door County's scenic places and ecological diversity, there has been significant effort in the last few decades to preserve some of the most ecologically sensitive, historic, and quintessentially Door County places. The Door County Land Trust and The Nature Conservancy of Wisconsin are working to protect many of these unique areas and have opened them to the public. State, federal, and local governments, including the Wisconsin Department of Natural Resources and the U.S. Fish and Wildlife Service, and the cities, towns, and villages also have a large number of parks and trails that are open to the public, most of which are free of charge. A multitude of private landowners have also allowed conservation easements across their land, including a few of the trails featured in this book.

Please do your best to protect these sensitive plant, animals, and the places in which they live. When you consider that millions of people visit Door County annually, even the smallest impact by each person can have a major aggregate effect on the region's rare plants and animals. We encourage you to support the organizations that make these places possible and respect the places you visit so that they may continue to be kept open for others to enjoy.

A BRIEF HISTORY

Door County's name originated from the Porte des Morts, a nickname from the French explorers who fished and trapped in these waters in the 1600s and heard tales from the local Potowatomi tribes about the perilousness of the "Death's Door" stretch of water between the Door Peninsula and Washington Island. The 1600s and 1700s were characterized by land swaps, trades, and battles among Potowatomi, Ho-Chunk, and a series of French Jesuit priests, trappers, explorers, and traders. Following the end of French control in 1763, the English took up fighting with the Potawatomi, and by the early 1800s, had all but extirpated the tribes. The Scandinavians followed, and by the mid-1800s, Door County was experiencing massive poputlation growth with new residents streaming in from Europe, the East Coast and from neighboring counties, with booming logging, fishing, mining, and trapping industries. The late 1800s brought tourism, with new resorts, campgrounds, and summer homes being built in numbers.

Today, Door County only has about 30,000 year-round residents, but remains a hugely popular tourist destination, drawing millions of visitors from around the country and around the world each summer. Visitors come to Door County for its outstanding natural beauty, cultural offerings, and cool summer temperatures.

Door County spans a wide variety of ecosystems, including sandy beaches, freshwater marshes, estuaries, bogs, and a diversity of forests. While agriculture is still the dominant industry in Door County, many parts of the peninsula are predominately forested, and if you spend any time in the woods, you will run across foundations of houses and barns, old stone walls, and brick kilns that suggest the past agricultural history of the region. In a few more rugged places, particularly along the Niagara Escarpment, you might also find massive old growth trees that managed to survive the agricultural period.

DOOR COUNTY PLACES

This book covers hiking trails around more than 25 communities in Door County, including Gardner, Namur, Brussels, Clay Banks, Maplewood, Forestville, Sturgeon Bay, Institute, Little Sturgeon Bay, Nasauwaupee, Egg Harbor, Fish Creek, Sevastopol, Carlsville, Jacksonport, Valmy, Ephraim, Sister Bay, Juddville, Gibralter, Baileys Harbor, Liberty Grove, Northport, Rowleys Bay, Ellison Bay, Gills Rock, and Washington.

Many visitors come by car from the south, crossing into Door County from Highway 42. As you slowly head north, the family farms and rolling oak savannahs along the southern border of the county near the tiny communities of Gardner, Namur, Brussels, Clay Banks, Maplewood, and Forestville begin to give way to the wetlands and beaches of the Shivering Sands.

The Shivering Sands region around Sturgeon Bay is one of the most ecologically rich areas in the Midwest. With its unique ridge and swale communities, left behind by the retreat of ancient glaciers, it contains many rare plants, animals and spectacular scenery.

As you continue north to Sturgeon Bay, Door County's only real "urban" area, you shouldn't miss stopping for lunch, groceries, or a walk around any of the local parks. The bridge itself, with views of lighthouses, the Sturgeon Bay ship canal, and the bustling center along the shores of Lake Michigan, makes this one of the highlights of any Door County roadtrip.

As your journey continues through towering forests and inland cherry orchards, you can head to the busier areas on the Green Bay side of the peninsula around Egg Harbor and Fish Creek or the quieter Lake Michigan side near Baileys Harbor. Whether on the Green Bay or along the Lake Michigan shoreline, these areas offer scenic vistas atop rocky bluffs, beaches, and other tourist attractions.

Even further north, on the Green Bay side, the many shops, restaurants, art galleries, cultural events, festivals, and abundant natural beauty of Ephraim and Sister Bay draw hundreds of thousands of visitors each year.

Further inland, as you near the top of the Peninsula around the township of Liberty Grove or the fishing communities of Ellison Bay, Northport, and Gills Rock, you'll find plenty of room to roam around the backroads and parks.

Taking the ferry north to Washington Island, or even up to Rock Island, you'll find a much quieter pace, well-suited for drives and bike trips along back roads and trips to the beach to take a dip in the cool waters of Lake Michigan on hot summer days.

HOW TO USE THIS BOOK

Common sense is always the best thing to bring with you any time you venture outdoors. Stories of tourists who fell off the side of the Grand Canyon trying to take a selfie, were gored trying to pet the bison in Yellowstone, or other human mishaps in the great outdoors are a staple of the local television station nightly news programs. In addition to snowmobiles going through ice, these generally fall into the following categories:

• Hikers who set out in shorts and t-shirts and got hypothermia after weather came in or got lost after it got dark and had to be rescued;

• Inland boaters and anglers who drowned because they were not wearing life jackets and may or may not have been drinking;

• Inexperienced sea kayakers, canoers, or standup paddleboarders who set out on Lake Michigan and drowned because they didn't have the skills to handle the weather, waves, tides, or current or were not wearing life jackets.

To avoid becoming news yourself, you need to know your own ability, bring enough warm clothes for weather, and keep an eye on where you're going. The following list includes a few caveats to get things started off on the right foot.

Level of Difficulty: Almost all of the trails in this book, with the exception of a few of the larger community forest tracts, are nothing more than walks in the woods. Most, if not all, of the trails we include in this book are completely doable for anyone who can climb a flight of stairs. Trails along the bluffs tend to be hillier, but even the harder trails are not difficult relative to Wisconsin. If you have any doubt about your preparedness and abilities, we encourage you to start out with the shorter trails on smaller parcels of land and go from there.

Public Access: The vast majority of Door County is private land. While many landowners are relaxed about access, particularly during the off-season, many second homeowners, farmers, and business owners are rightfully quite intolerant of trespassers. This book aims to be as specific as possible in providing directions to trails, but sometimes these involve easements across private land. When in doubt, ask permission, and if permission is denied, respect the landowner's right to his or her private property.

As a general rule, along Lake Michigan, Kangaroo Lake, and Europe Lake, the public has a right to access the beaches via public roads, public boat ramps, and public beaches. From those public access points, you may then walk along the beaches on all lands below the high-water mark. This does not include private access roads, stairways, docks, or backyards of private property, and you cannot cut through private property to get from a public road to the beach. On streams and rivers, the public is permitted to wade or launch boats at public road crossings or rights of way.

Paddling: Door County offers some of the best kayaking, canoeing, and standup paddleboard (SUP) opportunities in the Midwest, whether you're a novice or an experienced paddler. If you're venturing offshore, we strongly recommend that advanced paddlers seek out detailed maps for offshore excursions and that beginners take advantage of guided trips with one of the many outfitters across the region. Kayak and SUP rentals can be found in many of the larger towns along the peninsula.

The inland lakes and creeks in the region, especially around Kangaroo Lake, Europe Lake, Mink River Estuary, and

Little Lake, are relatively protected for novice kayaking, canoeing and SUP, and can offer exceptional wildlife viewing opportunities. Newer paddlers looking to get out on the water should sign up for a guided trip with one of the many tour companies. However, those venturing offshore should consult detailed maps, bring appropriate gear and provisions, and take normal safety precautions. The areas along the coast can be treacherous at any time of the year, so be cautious and use your head. Even on calmer inland ponds and rivers, boaters are required to have personal floatation devices (PFDs) under state law. Consult with the Wisconsin Department of Natural Resources for more information on rules and regulations, including boat licenses, fishing licenses, and PFD rules. When in doubt, if you're operating a watercraft under your own power, wear a lifejacket.

Hunting: Hunting is a cornerstone of Wisconsin outdoor heritage. The White-tailed Deer, Wild Turkey, and waterfowl seasons attract hunters from all over Wisconsin and neighboring states. While it is illegal to discharge firearms near residential dwellings, many of the sites included in this book are open to hunting, and seasons generally run in the fall, with an additional spring Wild Turkey hunt. Many Door County Land Trust and town properties allow hunting. In addition, some private landowners also allow hunters onto their property to hunt, particularly during the White-tailed Deer seasons. Anyone planning to spend time outdoors in Wisconsin, especially in the fall, should check the Wisconsin Department of Natural Resources website and become familiar with hunting season schedules. During hunting season, avoid areas with thick vegetation, wear at least two articles of blaze orange clothing, make noise, and be especially cautious in areas where you see hunters or empty trucks parked on roadsides.

Insects: Northern Wisconsin has a well-deserved reputation for biting insects. Door County is not nearly as bad as some other parts of the state, but mosquitoes still can be thick at times. West Nile Virus, Eastern Equine Encephalitis, and other mosquito-borne diseases have been reported. Door County also has large numbers of biting deer flies, which have a nasty reputation and tend to be found in high concentrations around standing freshwater and slowly moving streams, particularly in the late spring and early summer. Ticks are also a major issue, especially during the warmer months. Lyme Disease is very prevalent in Wisconsin, and other tick-borne diseases have also been reported. Hikers in wooded or grassy areas should avoid wearing shorts. We cannot emphasize enough the importance of taking general precautions like tucking your pants into your socks, spraying with strong insect repellent containing DEET, wearing long sleeves, and doing regular tick checks after hiking.

Animals: Door County is home to a wide variety of mammals. Some species, including rodents and bats, occasionally find their way into human dwellings. Give wild animals the wide berth they deserve, and enjoy them from a distance. While generally rare, rabies is known to occur in Wisconsin. Bats, raccoons, foxes, and skunks are some of the most common animals to contract rabies. Be cautious of any animal that approaches you, acts sick, or staggers, particularly if that animal is out during broad daylight. Report any sick animals to local law enforcement.

Invasive Plants: Dozens of non-native invasive plants have been introduced across Door County. Invasives can wreak havoc with local ecosystems, where they outcompete native plants. Brush off boots and clothes before and after hiking to avoid spreading seeds and consider participating in regular volunteer events to remove invasive species, including those hosted by the Door County Invasive Special Council and the Door County Land Trust.

Emergency Preparedness: Most parts of Door County are far from being a wilderness. Hikers are seldom more than a few miles from a road; there is good cellular coverage throughout the region; trails are generally short and well-marked. Don't be lulled into a false sense of security, however. Weather can change rapidly, and this part of Wisconsin is prone to unpredictable summer storms, high winds, spring and fall blizzards, fog, sudden drops in temperature, and even the occasional rare tornado. Take adequate precautions when venturing out. This means preparing for weather, bringing enough water, and telling someone where you're going. A first aid kit, snacks, GPS, warm clothes, rain jacket, and a cell phone are always a good idea even on the warmest summer days.

Maps: This book includes a selection of maps to help you find and enjoy some of Door County's best natural attractions. These maps are not comprehensive, however, and we urge you to consult park maps and trailhead signs for local trail maps.

General Safety and Property Crime. Door County is for the most part a very safe place. However, you should always use common sense when you are out in the field. In an urbanized area, nature preserves provide convenient, out of the way places for unlawful activities. Trailhead parking lots are also an easy target for property crime. Lock your valuables in the trunk of your car, or take them with you.

DOOR COUNTY NATURAL HISTORY

People come to Door County to experience the rejuvenating camaraderie of nature and get away from the grind of urban life. Whether you're a botanist or a casual hiker who simply likes to smell the flowers, a basic knowledge of the area's geology, plants, animals, and birds can greatly enhance your appreciation of this region's considerable natural beauty. This chapter will help you make a closer acquaintance with Door County's topography, wildlife, and changing seasons. Hopefully this knowledge will deepen your respect for the earth's natural cycles and complex inter-relationships and underscore the importance of treading lightly in this highly visited and sensitive part of the world.

"Ecological communities" is the phrase most often used by scientists to describe a group of species, plants, flowers, trees, insects, animals, birds, and the like, that live in the same place and interact with one another. Over the years, Wisconsin Department of Natural Resources ecologists have come up with some general names that describe certain collections of plants and animals. These general categories are used to characterize the plants and animals living in a particular area. Keep in mind that no two sites are exactly the same, and the ecological community is just a general guide to what kinds of plants and animals you might find in a given area. The following sections include descriptions of the community types most frequently encountered along the Lake Michigan coast. This list doesn't include all of the community types, but this will give you a general idea of what to expect and where to look for certain species.

Northern Dry Mesic Forest: This community, dominated by White Pine, Red Pine, Red Maple, and Red Oak, is dominant in Door County. Many areas have fern dominated understories and in lower spots seasonal wetlands known as vernal pools. Northern Dry Mesic Forests tend to be associated with sandy soils although not sand plains. Understory plants may also include Wild Sarsaparilla and Canada Mayflower. Animals found in Northern Dry Mesic Forests include Wild Turkey, Hermit Thrush, Ruffed Grouse, Eastern Bluebird, Brown-headed Cowbird, Gray Squirrel, and Porcupine. Examples of this community can be found throughout the area covered in this book and is widespread on private residential lands around Door County's cities and towns.

Northern Mesic Forest: The Northern Mesic Forest

community is widespread in smaller pockets in Door County. This community is dominated by trees like Sugar Maple, Eastern Hemlock, and often American Beech, particularly near the coast, along with tree species such as Basswood, Sugar Maple, Red Maple, Mountain Maple, Yellow Birch, Paper Birch, and White Ash, with more dominant coverage by Red Oak and White Pine. In some parts of the Door County, particularly those without large White-tailed Deer populations, there are dense layers of forest floor plants, including Canada Yew and Canada Mayflower. Animals of Northern Mesic Forests include Wood Frog, Meadow Vole, American Marten, Raccoon, Red Fox, Wild Turkey, Gray Squirrel, Snowshoe Hare, American Redstart, Red-eyed Vireo, Great-crested Flycatcher, and American Robin. Examples of this community can be found throughout the area covered in this book and is widespread on private residential lands around Door County's cities and towns.

Northern Wet-Mesic Forest: This forest type is found interspersed within other hardwood forest communities in Door County and is more commonly found in more northern latitudes. Characteristic trees include Balsam Fir, Black Ash, Tamarack, Paper Birch, and, in the northernmost and higher elevation reaches of the area this book covers, White Spruce and Black Spruce. This community may also have sedge meadows dominated by Soft-leaf Sedge and Three-seeded Sedge in wetter areas, as well as plants like Blunt-leaved Orchid and Heart-leaved Twayblade. Also look for understory plants, including Canada Mayflower, Wild Sarsaparilla, Wood Fern, and Yellow Trout Lily. Common animal and bird species include Red Squirrel, Ruffed Grouse, Red-breasted Nuthatch, Spotted Salamander, Canada Warbler, Porcupine, American Mink, Blue-spotted Salamander, and White-tailed Deer.

Red Maple Hardwood Swamp: This community is characterized by forested wetlands dominated by trees including Black Ash, Red Maple, Grey Birch, and Green

Ash, often in association with Balsam Fir and occasionally Alder species. Red Maple Hardwood Swamp forests only occur in fragmented, isolated stands in Door County. This community typically has wet understory, including Sphagnum Moss, Bluejoint, Cerex sedges and a variety of native ferns including Interrupted Fern, Royal Fern, and Sensitive. Animals found in Red Maple Hardwood Swamps include Northern Waterthrush, Wood Duck, Raccoon, White-tailed Deer, Silver-haired Bat, Spotted Salamander, Red-eyed Vireo, and Grey Catbird.

Hemlock Hardwood Swamp: This community is characterized by forested wetlands dominated by trees including Red Maple, Eastern Hemlock, and Yellow Birch. Hemlock Hardwood Swamp forests only occur in fragmented, isolated stands in Door County. This community typically includes an understory of Cinnamon Fern, Marsh Fern, Royal Fern, Three-seeded Sedge, and Long Sedge. Animals found in Hemlock Hardwood Swamps include Wood Duck, Wood Frog, Spring Peeper, Spotted Salamander, Blue-spotted Salamander, and Blanding's Turtle.

DOOR COUNTY OUTDOOR YEAR

No matter the month, you can find a quiet place along the coast of Door County to experience the magic of nature. Certainly, the summer is the most popular time to visit Door County. The woods, meadows, and marshes are alive with breeding songbirds and butterflies, and the warm days beckon visitors to the beaches. You may have to look a bit harder, but visitors searching for summer solitude can be sure to find it at many of the locations in this book.

As the locals know, the off-season, particularly the fall, has pleasant weather and far fewer crowds. In the fall, autumn leaves crunch underfoot, migrating birds flock overhead, and small mammals bustle about, stocking up for a long winter. Winter has its own appeal, especially if you're enjoying its stark beauty by cross-country ski or snowshoe. You may catch a glimpse of a white Snowshoe Hare, hear the scolding call of a Black-capped Chickadee from the top of a bare Red Maple, watch rafts of scoters diving for mollusks just off shore, or listen to the chitter of a Red Squirrel stirring from its nest on a sunny day.

Spring brings lots of rain, and with it the forests, beaches, and wetlands awake from the winter slumber. By March and April the trees start showing signs of life, and each day brings new arrivals of the season, including spring peepers in the woods, Red-winged Blackbirds singing in the marshes, Canada Geese, Tundra Swans, and Sandhill Cranes on the move, and the snow slowly melting off.

This section is a month-by-month guide to what you can expect to see, hear, and experience in the natural world in Door County.

January & February

These months are typically cold and snowy. While lakeshore areas are generally warmer than inland parts of Door County, the shorelines still occasionally register icy temperatures and lots of snow. Sunny January and February days are ideal for exploring the area's land trust preserves and back roads by cross-country ski or snowshoe. Look for tracks of small rodents, Ermine, Gray Fox, Red Fox, Fisher, Cottontail Rabbit, White-tailed Deer, and Raccoon in the snow. During these months, large rafts of ducks, including Long-tailed Duck, White-winged Scoter, Black Scoter, Greater Scaup, and Surf Scoter can be abundant in nearshore areas. Look for Bohemian Waxwings in flocks of Cedar Waxwings, particularly around ornamental plants in urban areas of Sturgeon Bay. Watch for Snowy Owls on the dunes and breakwaters especially along Green Bay and Chambers Island. At feeders, winter finches, including Evening Grosbeaks, Common and Hoary Redpolls, and Pine Siskins, may be present in significant numbers.

White-winged Crossbills may also appear in conifer forests and edges. On warm days, Red Squirrels and Chipmunks may be active, particularly around backyard feeders.

March

Early March brings the arrival of the first spring birds. The "kon-kaa-ree" of Red-winged Blackbirds is a welcome sound early in the month, with flocks of Common Grackles following shortly thereafter. As waterways start to thaw, the calls of Killdeer herald warmer days. By late March, the ice and snow loosen their winter grip, though temperatures remain cool, and migrant waterfowl float in large rafts in ocean bays and off promontories. Toward the end of the month, American Woodcocks "peent" and sky-dance in woodland clearings, and Silver Maple and Skunk Cabbage begin to flower.

April

By early April, Ruffed Grouse drum from downed logs and stumps, Northern Spring Peepers peep from thawed pond edges and wetlands, and Eastern Phoebes have returned to their nesting grounds. Wterfowl like Canada Geese and Sandhill Cranes are flying over to points north. As the ice leaves smaller wetlands, look for salamanders migrating across roads and trails to reach these ponds. Woodchucks and Eastern Chipmunks begin to emerge, and caterpillars explore the resurgent vegetation. Northern Leopard Frogs call, and Song Sparrows, Eastern Meadowlarks, Tree Swallows, and Chimney Swifts return. By mid-April, as flying insects become more numerous, the first bats of the season begin winging across the evening sky. The first warblers of spring, the Yellow-rumped and Pine Warblers, start arriving in numbers. As April comes to a close, ice disappears from the lakes, rivers, and wetlands. A multitude of plants poke their way through the ground, Eastern Garter Snakes slither in the grass, migrant songbirds begin to arrive, and Mourning Cloak and American Lady Butterflies flutter through the spring air.

May

In early May, everything seems to spring to life along the peninsula. Eastern Painted Turtles dig out of the mud from hibernation, and Red Maple and Gray Birch begin flowering with fuzzy catkins. Returning Winter Wrens sing from dense forests, and Green Frogs croak from wetlands. The second and third weeks in May are noteworthy, not only for the budding vegetation, but for the numbers of migrant wood warblers buzzing from every tree, searching for caterpillars. On a good mid-May day, a walk in the woods, particularly in migrant traps like the Ridges Sanctuary, might yield up to 20 or more warbler species, all in brilliant breeding plumage. By mid-to-late May, you can spot Monarch and Eastern Tiger Swallowtail Butterflies and hear American Toads croak. Great White Trillium flowers and Jack-in-the-Pulpit abound in the woodlands, and, toward the end of the month, most waterways are free of ice, and mosquitoes (and dreaded blackflies) start buzzing in decent numbers. Fruit trees flower, and many mammals and birds begin breeding. On the beaches, listen for the familiar cries of returning gulls and terns, Caspian Terns, Ring-billed Gulls, Herring Gulls, and Common Terns, as they forage on small fish in falling tides.

June

The beginning of June is still cool in Door County, with even cooler nights, but the throng of tourists from the south is a reminder that it is officially summer. A walk in the woods will be accompanied by the sounds of warblers defending their breeding territories. Baltimore Orioles build pendulous nests from overhanging branches; Rose-breasted Grosbeaks sing and chip in the forests; Indigo Buntings twitter from their perches, and Great-crested Flycatchers sound from the treetops. The first White-tailed Deer fawns are born around mid-month, and the lush carpet of ferns, including Royal Fern, Cinnamon Fern, and Interrupted Fern, begins to blanket the forest floor. Pitcher Plants abound in wet forests. By mid-June, the marshes are alive with nesting Painted Turtles, Common Yellowthroats, Eastern Willets, and Song Sparrows, while Pitcher Plants flower and marsh plants grow tall. On the offshore islands in Green Bay, Piping Plovers are nesting, and Caspian and Common Tern colonies are going full swing.

July

Early July brings an influx of summer visitors to Door County, and the woods and marshes abound with blooming wild flowers and meadow plants like Wild Sarsparilla, Ramps, Indian Pipe, Cranberry, Queen Anne's Lace, and Wood Lily. Purple Loosestrife, an invasive species, blooms from ditches, roadsides, and wetlands, while butterflies descend on the meadows to feast. By mid-July the songbirds are quieter as they focus energy on feeding their young. Gulls and terns soar over beaches and estuaries, where they hunt for fish to bring back to chicks at the offshore colonies. Grassland birds have fledged, and parent birds are busy teaching the young of the year how to fend for themselves. Shorebirds are also on the move, returning from their short Arctic breeding season. Look for increasing numbers of Semipalmated and Least Sandpiper along the shorelines.

August

The summer season is in full swing by August, and with temperatures increasing, visitors begin to flock to the beaches. Meadow plants like Little Bluestem, Common Goldenrod, Forest Goldenrod, Dusty Goldenrod, Cardinal Flower, and Closed Gentian flower draw in butterflies to forage. Wetlands continue buzzing with dragonflies, including Autumn Meadowhawk and Spotted Spreadwing. Tadpoles emerge as full-grown Wood Frogs, and you can spot small families of Wood Ducks, Common Goldeneye, and Common Merganser with rapidly growing offspring in forested wetlands. Turkey hens are in the woodlands with troops of growing young birds called polts. Gulls and terns soar over beaches and estuaries. August temperatures are variable; some years see days in the 80s and 90s, while in others the mercury stays in the 60s during the day and dips into the 40s at night. Toward the end of the month, Monarch butterflies and Ruby-throated Hummingbirds start their fall migrations southward, as numbers of Arctic breeding shorebirds swell along the mudflats.

September

September mornings are crisp, a harbinger of cold weather to come. Goldenrod and other meadow plants continue to bloom, and Little Bluestem and Gentian also begin to flower in large numbers drawing butterflies like Red Admiral. Flocking blackbirds begin to appear, particularly around farms and marshes. By mid-to- late September, deciduous forests across Door County begin to show the first hints of orange, gold, and red. By month's end, Blue Jays are more noticeable in large, noisy migrant flocks, and other breeding birds, like White-throated Sparrow and Yellow-rumped Warbler, start moving south from their northern breeding grounds to migrate through in considerable numbers. Toward the end of the month, watch for large flocks of Tree Swallows swarming in the mashes as they move south for the winter.

October

Door County's fall colors are at their peak around mid-October, depending on precipitation and temperature and draw huge crowds of visitors all month. The first snow and hard freeze of the season usually occur in October, though exact dates vary. Fall Wild Turkey and White-tailed Deer hunting seasons typically start around the beginning of October, and hunters take to the woods. By the month's end all but the last of the Neotropical migrants and summer crowds have gone south, leaving the human winter population to breathe a collective sigh of relief from the hectic pace of the tourist season. Turtles and frogs tuck into the mud for winter hibernation as the temperatures start to dip, and the last of the migrant songbirds move through en route to warmer climes. Tamarack is in full yellow color toward the middle of the month. Migrant birds like White-crowned and Fox Sparrow start moving southward by mid-month, while flocks of winter residents like Dark-eyed Junco and American Tree Sparrow begin to appear toward the end of the month.

November

By early November, Sugar Maples, American Beech, Shagbark Hickory, and a few species of oak still have color, though other species have long since dropped their leaves. Eastern Painted Turtles and Mourning Cloak Butterflies take their last opportunities to bask in the sun on warm early November days. Intermediate Wood Fern may still remain green, peeking out from the early snowfalls. By the beginning of November, chipmunks have begun to hibernate, Gray Squirrels finish their nests and stash nuts for the cold winter ahead, and other small mammals and rodents disappear to warmer nooks. The first large flocks of the wintering waterfowl begin to appear along the coast with Red-necked Grebe, Red-breasted Merganser, Long-tailed Duck, Common Eider, and three species of scoter rafting offshore. Other winter resident birds, including Pine Siskins and American Tree Sparrows, appear in larger flocks at feeders alongside resident species.

Late November & December

Late November and December herald another in influx of winter visitors, drawn to Door County for cross-country skiing, snowshoeing, and snowmobiling. The weather can be variable. In some years, winter begins in earnest. Leaves fall off the trees, and many shallow ponds, wetlands, and bays freeze. In other years, sunny, warmer days persist as autumn draws to a close. As winter progresses, larger bodies of water begin to freeze. Watch for the Northern Lights on cloudless nights. Snowy Owls may appear along the lakeshore, particularly on dunes and breakwaters and along frozen agricultural fields. Snowshoe Hare and Ermine have turned white for the year. Watch for Ravens flocking and for the return of wintering Rough-legged Hawks and Northern Shrikes patrolling over open fields. At feeders, look for the first of the winter finches to appear, including Evening Grosbeaks, Common and Hoary Redpolls, and Pine Siskins.

The Southern Door and Clay Banks

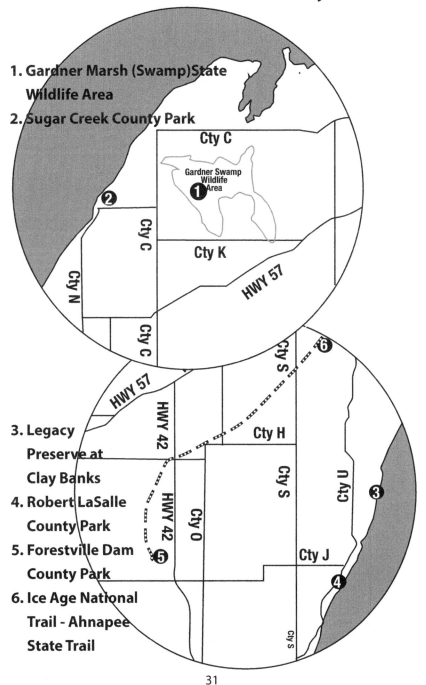

1. Gardner Marsh (Swamp)State Wildlife Area
2. Sugar Creek County Park

3. Legacy Preserve at Clay Banks
4. Robert LaSalle County Park
5. Forestville Dam County Park
6. Ice Age National Trail - Ahnapee State Trail

CHAPTER 1.

THE SOUTHERN DOOR AND CLAY BANKS

Gardner, Namur, Brussels, Clay Banks,
Maplewood, and Forestville

The Southern Door and Clay Banks region, south of
Sturgeon Bay, includes the farming hamlets of Gardner,
Namur, and Brussels and the settlements of Clay Banks,
Maplewood, and Forestville. From the red clay cliffs along
Lake Michigan, once used by early sailors for navigation,
to the farm fields, red barns and pastures, this region is
distinctly different from what you might expect when you
think of Door County. The area was originally settled by
the Chippewa and Menomonie tribes, and in the 1850s saw
a large influx of European settlers, drawing loggers from
Scandinavia and Germany and farmers from Belgium.
The early settlers began to clear Door County's vast forests, hauling trees by barge down the Ahnapee River to a
sawmill in the center of Forestville. Along the lake at Clay
Banks, at what is now Legacy Preserve at Clay Banks, they
built a shipping dock and several clay brick manufacturing
facilities. Inland, as the land was cleared, farmers began
to settle family farms, bringing dairy cows and silage crops
to this part of the state.

Today, driving the country roads past fields of wheat and
dairy herds, you'll be reminded of Belgium and Scandinavia when you look at the names of the roads and on mail-
boxes. While the brick factories and sawmills are gone,
today the area looks much the same as it would have in the
late 1800s—with red clay banks along the lake and family
farms inland. The Southern Door and Clay Banks have a
very different feel from the rest of Door County, with oak
savannahs and farms that look more like the southern part
of the state. The fall colors of these oak woodlots around
farms in this area are the stuff of dreams for landscape

photographers and anyone who enjoys rural country landscapes. This region is perfect for a long walk or bike ride down low-traffic roads or trails, no matter the season.

Few day-trippers and hikers stop to explore the Southern Door and Clay Banks on their way to points north because this area lacks the tourist attractions and scenic woodlands of areas north of the Sturgeon Bay Bridge. However, if you pause a while to enjoy the rural charm, you'll find a spot without the crowds and a true flavor of rural Wisconsin life. If you're truly looking to get off the main tourist tracks and explore the real quiet side of Door County, the Southern Door and Clay Banks area is a great choice.

1. Gardner Marsh (Gardner Swamp) State Wildlife Area

Southwest of Sturgeon Bay you'll find a large state-owned area of wild lands, which the locals call Gardner Swamp. It is better known by its official name—Gardner Marsh State Wildlife Area and is regionally famous for its diversity and abundance of wildlife. Gardner Marsh boasts some of the most extensive oak woodlands in Door County, which reach their northern range in the Southern Door, along with American Elm, American Beech, Hemlock and Sugar Maple, and this area contains extensive wetlands interspersed with Northern Hardwood forests along Kayes Creek, perfect for breeding and migrating ducks and geese.

The Wisconsin Department of Natural Resources (WDNR) manages about 1,200 acres in this area for White-tailed Deer, Wild Turkey, and waterfowl hunting. The Door County Land Trust (DCLT) manages another 400 acres for conservation as part of its Brussels Hill and Kayes Creek Preserve. The land trust preserves are open from time to time for tours through the land trust, but otherwise lack public access. The state lands have rustic trails, primarily used by hunters and trappers. This is a wild place, and at all seasons, spray for ticks, which may be abundant. During

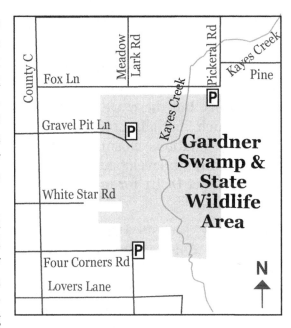

the hunting seasons, make sure to don your blaze orange. However, if you're looking for solitude and have a healthy sense of direction, Gardner Swamp is worth a few hours of your time.

As you'd expect from an area managed for hunting, it is a great place to find Wild Turkey, Ruffed Grouse, Wood Duck, Sandhill Crane, and White-tailed Deer. In addition to waterfowl, deer, and Wild Turkey hunting opportunities, Gardner Marsh is best a breeding location for Hine's Emerald and other dragonflies, Northern Spring Peeper, and Chorus Frogs. There are large areas of Emergent and Submergent cattail marshes along Kayes Creek, bordered by mature Northern Mesic Forests on the WDNR parcels. On the Door County Land Trust parcels, you'll also find steep ravines bordering drier upland Northern Dry Mesic Forests around Brussels Hill. This area can be outstanding for songbird migration in the spring and fall, where you can find a variety of migrating wood warblers including Canada, Nashville, Bay-breasted, and Blackpoll. Golden-winged Warblers are thought to breed here. With the abundance of mature oak trees, the fall colors can be spectacular.

Trails, Access & Facilities: There are no facilities. The WDNR tract is open to the public and has a network of rustic trails, but these are often overgrown or not maintained much, if at all. Contact WDNR for information on hunting regulations, closures, and access. The DCLT sites are currently undeveloped and accessible by permission only. Contact DCLT for information on access, including organized walks.

Contact: Wisconsin Department of Natural Resources http://www.dnr.state.wi.us/. Door County Land Trust http://www.doorcountylandtrust.org/. There is a parking area at the end of Gravel Pit Road, about 9401 Gravel Pit Rd., Gardner, WI 54204, another parking area at the end of Pickeral Road at about 2899 Pickeral Rd., Brussels, WI 54204, and a third parking area past the intersection of Four Corners Road and Hilly Ridge Road at about 3550 Four Corners Rd., Brussels, WI 54204. No fee.

2. Sugar Creek County Park

Best known for its smelt fishery, Sugar Creek County Park has a small boat ramp, accessible when the lake levels are appropriate, and a picnic area. There are no formal trails but plenty of grassy lawns and Northern Mesic woods for a quick jaunt and spot to stretch your legs. The park's forty wooded acres sit along Green Bay. In addition to the boat launch and fishing opportunities, the big draw here is for winter storm watching—the exposed location of the park makes it a popular spot to watch big waves rolling off Green Bay when conditions are right.

Wildlife watchers will find this a good spot for migrating raptors in the spring and fall, notably Broad-winged Hawks, which may migrate through in large flocks known as 'kettles,' as well as migrating songbirds. In the winter months, the mouth of Sugar Creek may host large rafts of diving ducks such as Greater Scaup and Surf Scoter, which dive down to

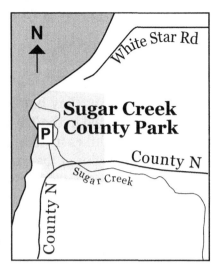

forage on zebra and quagga mussels growing at bottom of the Green Bay. If you have waders, or don't mind getting your feet wet, you can also use the park as a jumping off point to explore the 10-mile long namesake Sugar Creek, which flows into the Green Bay at the park and is popular when the smelt are running. Local breeding birds include Chipping Sparrow, Red-eyed Vireo, and American Robin, along with often abundant Canada Geese out on the bay.

Trails, Access & Facilities: Sugar Creek County Park has parking, restrooms, a boat launch, a picnic area with grills, and lake access.

Contact: Door County Parks System, http://map.co.door. wi.us/parks/. 2393 White Star Rd., Brussels, WI 54202. No fee.

3. Legacy Preserve at Clay Banks

Legacy Preserve at Clay Banks, also known as the Kreuter Preserve, is located in the Town of Clay Banks and is one of the most scenic hikes in all of Door County. The short 1.0-mile loop trail begins at the parking area, at the top of a large red clay bank along Lake Michigan. The trail, though short, is steep in places, with some sandy soils that can cause slips

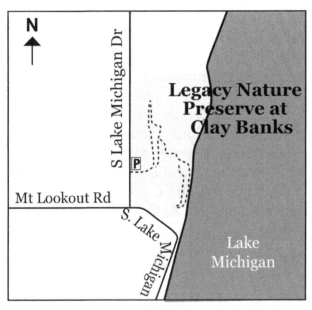

and slides. The trail traverses down the hill through native prairie and shrublands and finally ends at the Lake Michigan shoreline, at a secluded, sandy Great Lakes Beach and Dune community with a small beach. The area was the site of a historic sawmill and timber shipping dock, homes, and a school more than 100 years ago, which you can see remnants of along the lakeshore. Today, the preserve is managed by the Door County Land Trust and includes about 3,000-feet of Lake Michigan shoreline.

At the beach, you'll have views of the red clay banks and rugged shoreline. This area with its sand banks and submerged rocks was considered treacherous in the days be-fore marine navigation equipment. There are parts of sev-eral historic shipwrecks visible offshore when lake levels are low. The preserve is also an excellent place to watch the sunrise from atop the promontory near the parking area or find solitude at the small, scenic, sandy beach. The Preserve includes pockets of Northern Wet Mesic and Northern Mesic Forest communities and wetlands areas and can be an excellent place for spring wildflowers. Look for breeding Black-throated Green Warbler, American Redstart, Coyote, and White-tailed Deer, as well as migrat-ing raptors in the spring and fall, diving ducks offshore in the colder months, and photo soaring Bald Eagles. In the prairie areas, watch for Clay-colored Sparrow, Bobolink, Eastern Meadowlark, Red Fox, Raccoon, Striped Skunk, and other smaller mammals.

Trails, Access & Facilities: There are no facilities. There is a 1.0-mile loop trail, which is steep in some parts, that leads from the parking area to the beach and back. Contact DCLT for more specific access information. Bikes, horses, and motorized vehicles are prohibited. Hunting is authorized pursuant to DCLT guidelines and permission.

Contact: Door County Land Trust, http://www.door-countylandtrust.org/. 1188 S. Lake Michigan Dr., Stur-geon Bay, WI 54235. Park along the shoulder of S. Lake Michigan Dr. or in the parking lot and hike east to access the preserve. No fee.

4. Robert La Salle County Park

As a monument to the early Great Lakes explorer who plied the waters of Lake Michigan in this area during the mid-1600s, Robert La Salle County Park lies just north of the

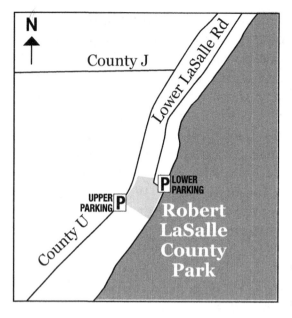

Kewaunee County border along Lake Michigan. The 25-acre park is popular with locals¬ for picnicking, sunbathing, and enjoying views of Lake Michigan. The parcels are owned and operated by the Door County Parks System. The park is situated along steep sand bluffs, which were created by rises and fall in Lake Michigan's water levels over geologic time. There is also a central ravine along Bear Creek, which runs along the park's boundary, several ephemeral creeks, and stands of Northern Mesic Forest.

While the park is primarily developed and does not offer much in the way of true hiking, this area offers public lakefront access in a stretch of Lake Michigan that is primarily private property, and if lake levels are low, you can walk at the high water mark along the rocky beach.

This is a great place to stop for an hour or two if you're in the area or looking for a public beach in an area surrounded largely by private land or want to check out some Great Lakes maritime history. The upper and lower sections of the park are connected with stairways, which provide access to the site's La Salle historical marker.

Trails, Access & Facilities: There are no formal trails. The park has a playground and restroom facilities.

Contact: Door County Parks System, http://map.co.door.wi.us/parks/. 408 County U, Algoma, WI 54201. No fee.

5. Forestville Dam County Park

Located in the Town of Forestville and gateway to the Ice Age Trail, the 79-acre Forestville Dam County Park, also known as Forestville Mill Pond Park, is a pleasant stop over point for exploring, especially with small kids in tow. While the park, owned and operated by the Door County Parks System, lacks trails itself, it is the perfect spot for picking up the Ahnapee portion of the Ice Age Trail. Recent dredging and wetlands restoration projects will restore the park to its former glory—a place for puttering around the mill pond in a canoe or kayak or casting a line. You can also walk along the dam and just enjoy this small piece of Door County outdoors.

This park is situated on the western banks of the Forestville Mill Pond, locally known as Forestville Flowage, a dammed stretch of the Ahnapee River, which is generally calm and flat at all times. The park is primarily developed with a boat

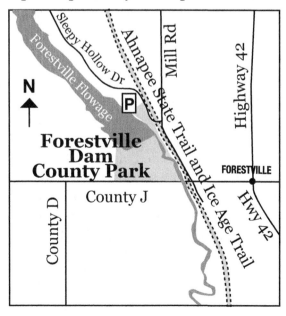

launch, dock, playground, and picnic facilities, but also contains wooded Northern Wet Mesic Forest areas with open grassy areas and playing fields. Look for Racoon, Black-capped Chickadee, American Goldfinch, Grey Squirrel, Chipping Sparrow, Chimney Swift, and Ruby-throated Hum-mingbird.

Trails, Access & Facilities: There are no formal trails. The park has a playground, dock, picnic area, and rest-room facilities.

Contact: Door County Parks System, http://map.co.door. wi.us/parks/. 475 Mill Rd., Forestville, WI 54235. This park and parking lot serve as a primary access point to the Ice Age National Trail and Ahnapee State Trail. No fee.

6. Ice Age National Trail - Ahnapee State Trail

One of the great national rails-to-trails projects, the Ice Age National Trail, runs along the Ahnapee State Trail, one of Wisconsin's premier examples of a rails-to-trails project. The trail was built along the railbed of the historic Ahnap-ee and Western Railroad, which earned its small place in history at the height of World War II when German POWs were sent via rail along this trail to Door County to work in the cherry orchards.

Developing this trail has been a collaborative effort of a large number of individuals and organizations over the years, and currently the Door County Parks System is the lead agency in maintaining the trail's Door County stretch-es. The 'co-branded' Ice Age National Trail - Ahnapee State Trail in this section of the state runs about 50 miles from Kewaunee County to Sturgeon Bay and then Penin-sula State Park. The trail is flat crushed limestone, ideally suited for a quiet walk or bike ride, and is great for families with small kids, including when you're pushing a stroller.

In the spring, summer, and fall, the trail is open to hik-ing, biking, and horseback riding. In the winter, cross-county skis and snowmobiles are the primary mode of transport. The trail spans just about all of southern Door County's interior community types, including Northern Wet Mesic, Northern Mesic, and Northern Dry Mesic forests, along with scattered pockets of wetlands and old fields. The trail is an excellent place to observe spring wildflowers and plants and animals that favor edges and disturbed successional communities, including Aspen stands and old fields. Par-

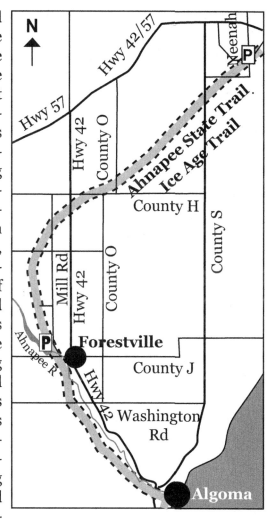

ticularly in the quiet early morning and at dusk watch for Wild Turkey, Monarch Butterfly, Mourning Warbler, Clay-colored Sparrow, White-tailed Deer, Spotted Salamander, Raccoon, Virginia Opossum, and Red Fox.

There are a number of places to access the trail, though one of the easiest is by parking at the trailhead parking lot located just south of downtown Sturgeon Bay off Neenah Ave. between Leeward St. and Wilson Rd. Easy access and parking is also available at Forestville Dam County Park.

The approximately 10.0-mile stretch from Forestville to Algoma is particularly nice. From Forestville County Park in Forestville, the trail initially follows the Ahanpee River south, crossing the river over a new bridge, giving you a bit of views of the river and Sturgeon Bay in the distance. You can trek as long as you'd like and then turn back around. The nice thing about the trail is that it is impossible to get lost, and you'll meet other fellow travelers who are similarly enjoying this quiet part of Door County.

Trails, Access & Facilities: The Ice Age National Trail and the Ahnapee State Trail is a well-maintained, graded rails-to-trails trail. There are 50 miles of trails from Peninsula State Park to Kewaunee County, and more sections are slated for addition in the coming years.

Contact: Website: Ahnapee State Trail, http://www.ahnapeetrail.org. Door County Parks System, http://map.co.door.wi.us/parks/. Kewaunee County Promotion and Recreation Dept., http://www.kewaunee.org/. Access the trail by parking at the trailhead parking lot located just south of downtown Sturgeon Bay off Neenah Ave. between Leeward St. and Wilson Rd., or at Forestville County Park, 475 Mill Rd., Forestville, WI 54235. No fee.

SHIVERING SANDS

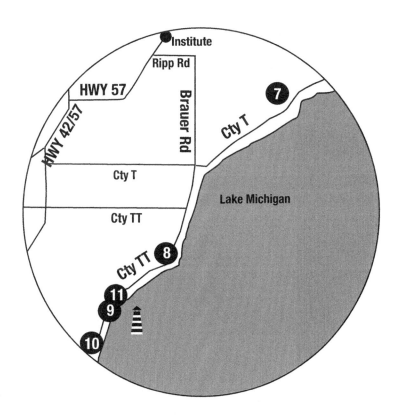

7. **Shivering Sands State Natural Area**
8. **Kellner Fen**
9. **Sturgeon Bay Ship Canel Nature Preserve and Lighthouse**
10. **Sturgeon Bay Ship Canel North Pierhead Light Walk**
11. **Portage Park**

CHAPTER 2.

SHIVERING SANDS

Sturgeon Bay, Institute, Clay Banks

One of the most ecologically important and scenic parts of Door County, the Shivering Sands region runs along the western edge of Lake Michigan, from the Sturgeon Bay Ship Canal in the south to Whitefish Dunes State Park in the north. The area is home to a large number of threatened and endangered species and some of the most strikingly beautiful landscapes in all of Wisconsin.

Originally settled by the Chippewa and Menomonie tribes, by the 1850s the area drew European settlers who built the Sturgeon Bay Ship Canal, bisecting the peninsula and providing a more convenient access to the port of Sturgeon Bay. By the 1920s, a local would-be developer named Oram Glidden had purchased most of the land between what is now Whitefish Dunes State Park and the present-day Sturgeon Bay Ship Canal.

Glidden eventually lost most of his fortune and died without realizing his dream of large-scale development in the area, but during the period from the 1930s through the 1990s, Glidden Lodge and a handful of homes along Glidden Drive were built. Aside from those areas, the Shivering Sands has retained much of its conservation value and character thanks to the Door County Land Trust, the Nature Conservancy, Ducks Unlimited, municipal governments, and other local landowners.

Today, you can get glimpses of the landscape along Glidden Drive, recognized by the state as a Wisconsin Rustic Road, and along the trails of the region we highlight in this chapter. For those interested in exploring the wildest areas of Door County, look no further than the Shivering Sands region.

7. Shivering Sands State Natural Area

The Shivering Sands State Natural Area is one of the most ecologically significant sites in Door County, comprising

dozens of natural community types over more than 6,000 acres. Shivering Sands State Natural Area includes the wetlands along Giesel Creek to the north, Dunes Lake, Lower Dunes Lake, and Shivering Sands Creek to the south, and other smaller ponds, bogs, fens, and lakes with peat, marl, loam, and dolomite bottoms. Especially noteworthy is the largest intact Northern White Cedar swamp in the state of Wisconsin and one of the largest in the United States. The area is unique in its complicated hydrology, with the wetlands and lakes fed by multiple springs and creeks and lots of ephemeral wet areas. These springs also drain the complex through fissures in the underlying dolomite bedrock.

A large section of this area is protected by The Nature Conservancy, along with the Door County Land Trust and other partners. The area is being actively managed for wildlife habitat, including restoration and dredging activities around Dunes Lake to promote habitat for breeding ducks and geese and removal of invasive species. Wetlands breeding birds, including Bald Eagle, Black Tern, Sand-hill Crane, Virginia Rail, Sora, and Osprey can be found, along with Hine's Emerald Dragonfly, Muskrat, Striped Skunk, Pygmy Shrew, Beaver, and occasionally River Otter. The diverse wetlands include Northern Sedge Meadows, Emergent and Submergent Marsh, Shrub Carr, and Fen communities. Closer to Lake Michigan, the adjacent Northern Wet Mesic and Northern Mesic Forests cover a substantial Great Lakes Ridge and Swale complex. In the spring and summer, look for wildflowers including Showy Lady's Slipper Orchid and Dwarf Lake Iris. The area also includes some significant sand dunes, which lend the name to the area.

Trails, Access & Facilities: This area, primarily west of Glidden Drive along Lake Michigan, is maintained as a natural area and lacks well developed trail systems. There are no facilities. The lakes, creek, and wetlands areas can be explored by kayak or canoe, by launching off the Dolan's Creek Bridge on Haberli Rroad around 4300 Haberli Road, Sevastopol, WI 54235. Park well off the shoulder of Haberli on either side of the bridge, and put in boats on the right side of the road. Proceed south along Dolan's Creek from the bridge. Foot access is restricted, and interested visitors should contact the Door County Land Trust or The Nature Conservancy for information on access and organized hikes.

Contact: Door County Land Trust, http://www.door-countylandtrust.org. The Nature Conservancy, http://www.nature.org. 4300 Haberli Rd., Sevastopol, WI 54235. No fee.

8. Kellner Fen State Natural Area

Kellner Fen State Natural Area, part of Cave Point-Clay Banks Great Lakes Ridge and Swale Complex, is an ecologically significant Shore Fen wetland complex, which includes a floating peat mat with a number of interconnected areas of open water surrounded by Northern Sedge Meadow, Northern Wet Mesic Forest and Northern Mesic Forest communities situated atop dolomite bedrock. This area includes a network of parcels owned and managed by Door County Land Trust, the Wisconsin Department of Natural Resources and The Nature Conservancy. The Door County Land Trust maintains a short 1.0-mile trail that crosses over several ridges and swales on the way to the edge of the fen. The trails are unlike anything else in Door County and really interesting to walk on, giving hikers a squishy, floating sensation with each step.

Kellner Fen has a number of uncommon and rare plants including Coast Sedge, spring orchids, Northern Bog Sedge, and Slender Bog Arrowgrass and is home to a diversity of plants and animals including Blanchard's Cricket Frog, Porcupine, Ruffed Grouse, Canada Warbler, Hine's Emerald Dragonfly, Black Bear, Striped Skunk, Fisher, and Snowshoe Hare. Kellner Fen is also a key wetland situated along the lake, providing an important stopover site for migrating waterfowl. This site can also be a good place for watching migrating raptors in the spring and fall when conditions are right.

The fen is just inland of the larger Cave Point-Clay Banks Great Lakes Ridge and Swale complex, which is situated between the fen and Lake Michigan. Though the fen has no natural outlet to Lake Michigan, several man-made canals were excavated during agricultural use of the property in the mid-1900s. Along Lake Michigan, across Lake

Forest Park Road, the Fen is bordered by tall, high, natural sand dunes and a rocky cobble and bedrock beach (not accessible from the trails).

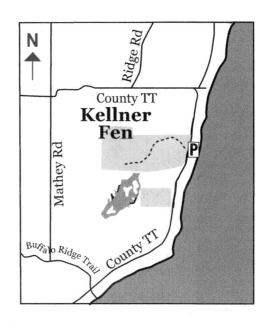

Trails, Access & Facilities: The preserve has no facilities. There is about 1.0-mile, roundtrip, of maintained trails on the DCLT parcels, which provides direct access to the fen. Waterproof footwear is a good idea, particularly during wetter parts of the year. Leashed dogs are permitted on the DCLT preserve. Bikes, horses, and motorized vehicles are prohibited. Hunting is authorized pursuant to DCLT guidelines and permission.

Contact: Door County Land Trust, http://www.doorcountylandtrust.org/. The Nature Conservancy, http://www.nature.org. Park off Lake Forest Park Rd. and follow the signs to the trailhead across from 3220 Lake Forest Park Rd., Sturgeon Bay, WI 54235. No fee.

9. Sturgeon Bay Ship Canal Recreation Area

With a network of 2.5 miles of flat, sandy trails, two historic lighthouses, views of the Sturgeon Bay Ship Canal, Lake Michigan vistas, and sandy beaches, the Sturgeon Bay Ship Canal Recreation Area is a local favorite. Considered part of the Shivering Sands complex, parcels on either side of the Sturgeon Bay Ship Canal contain a significant Great Lakes Ridge and Swale formation just inland of a large Great Lakes Beach and Dune community.

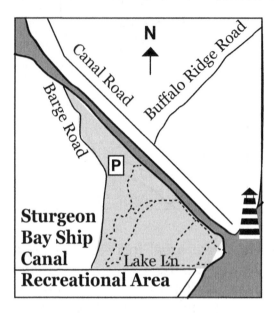

In the late 1800s, the Sturgeon Bay Ship Canal was built right through the Great Lakes Ridge and Swale formation in an effort to create a faster and less dangerous route between the port of Green Bay and Lake Michigan. In later years, this area was extensively farmed, which included dredging and excavation of additional trenches and channels. Today, the Door County Land Trust, in cooperation with The Nature Conservancy, the City of Sturgeon Bay, Sturgeon Bay Utilities, and other partners, are protecting and restoring this area's ecological communities, including the Ridge and Swale formation along the Ship Canal and nearby Strawberry Creek.

Look for forests of Northern Mesic and Northern Dry Mesic trees, interspersed with wet swales and dry ridges, that contain a number of rare plants including Dwarf Lake Iris, Dune Thistle, and Dune Goldenrod. Further inland, the canal passes through an ancient lakebed that was once part of Lake Michigan. This is an excellent area for finding migrant birds during late spring.

A great sandy beach and views of the lighthouses are best accessed from the Town of Sturgeon Bay parking lot at the end of Lake Lane. You can also pick up the trails from the Door County Land Trust parking lot, also along Lake Lane. From the end of Lake Lane, there are also excellent views of the Sturgeon Bay Ship Canal Lighthouse and the North Pierhead Light, the U.S. Coast Guard facility, and the canal itself. Trails are generally flat and sandy and can provide a good workout tramping through the sandy spots and beach.

Trails, Access & Facilities: There are no facilities. Most of the trails in this area, including along the edges of the Ship Canal, have white DCLT markers, although an informal network of trails is also established. Contact DCLT for more specific trail information.

Contact: Door County Land Trust, http://www.door-countylandtrust.org/. The Nature Conservancy, http://www.nature.org. The Recreation Area lies north of Lake Ln. with private and DCLT property to the south, accessible from parking lots at 5340 Lake Ln., Sturgeon Bay, WI 54235 or 5200 Lake Ln., Sturgeon Bay, WI 54235. No fee.

10. U.S. Coast Guard Station and Sturgeon Bay Ship Canal-North Side

For a truly unusual hike, not for the faint of heart, visitors can walk out to the end of the 1,200-foot long North Pierhead into Lake Michigan at the mouth of the Sturgeon Bay Ship Canal. The North Pierhead is about 10 feet wide, with an arching metal infrastructure overhead, and should only be attempted in calm weather. At the very end of the North Pierhead is the striking red North Pierhead Light (closed to the public). This site has long been used as a navigation point and landmark in Door County.

In 1881, after the Sturgeon Bay Ship Canal officially opened,

construction began on the original lighthouse, pierheads, and U.S. Coast Guard buildings. Today, the canal is still used for shipping, under authority of the U.S. Army Corps of Engineers, and the two lighthouses, the North Pierhead Light and the Sturgeon Bay Ship Canal Lighthouse, still operate. A small U.S. Coast Guard station sits at the mouth of the Ship Canal. The station is staffed year-round, and operations focus on search and rescue, law enforcement, and cold-water rescue missions in Lake Michigan. As a working Coast Guard Station, public entry into buildings and lighthouses is prohibited, subject to U.S. Coast Guard Station rules and regulations; however, the public is allowed access to the North Pierhead. The end of the North Pierhead offers panoramic views of Lake Michigan, Lily Bay, and Whitefish Point to the north, down to Kewaunee County in the south, and excellent views of both lighthouses, the Ship Canal, and the Coast Guard Station. Though rarely crowded, this is a popular spot for lighthouse aficionados and maritime history buffs.

Trails, Access & Facilities: There are no facilities. Park only in designated areas. The walkout on the North Pierhead is about 0.3-miles roundtrip. Access and closures are subject to U.S. Coast Guard rules and regulations. The Door County Maritime Museum runs annual lighthouse tours, including to these lighthouses, each summer.

Contact: United States Coast Guard Station-Sturgeon Bay, http://www.uscg.mil/d9/sectLakeMichigan/STASturgeonBay.asp. Park in the U.S. Coast Guard Station's visitor parking lot on the south side of Canal Rd. at 2501 Canal Rd., Sturgeon Bay, WI 54235 No fee.

11. Portage Park

The Town of Sturgeon Bay operates tiny Portage Town Park. Though small, and without formal trails, this park packs a punch for its views of Lake Michigan, the Sturgeon Bay Ship Canal, the U.S. Coast Guard Station, and lighthouses. Even during the busiest months, this park is generally empty, unknown to all but a few locals, and depending on lake levels, you may have the sandy, expansive beaches to yourself for a nice walk. The park forms a natural point into Lake Michigan and during migration is a good

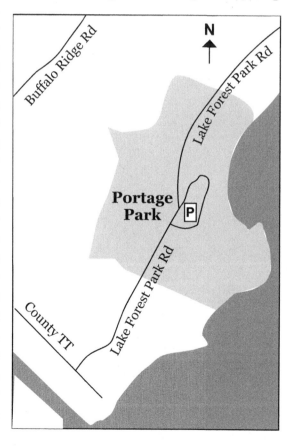

place to watch for migrant raptors such as Broad-winged Hawks, waterfowl, and songbirds as they follow the Lake Michigan shoreline. In the winter this can be an excellent spot for wintering diving ducks including Greater Scaup, Common Goldeneye, Redhead, Long-tailed Duck, and Common and Red-breasted Mergansers.

Trails, Access & Facilities: Portage Park has a small parking area and beach access. This site also provides access to other beaches to the north (Kickapoo Dr. Beach, Winnebago Dr. Beach, Chippewa Dr. Beach) and to the south (Sturgeon Bay Canal Recreation Area) below the high-water mark. Watch carefully for the sign to the park, as it is easy to miss.

Contact & Directions: Owned and operated by the Township of Sturgeon Bay. Look for the entrance marked with a large boulder with a plaque indicating the park's name, at 2650 Lake Forest Park Rd., Sturgeon Bay, WI 54235. No fee.

CHAPTER THREE

STURGEON BAY AREA

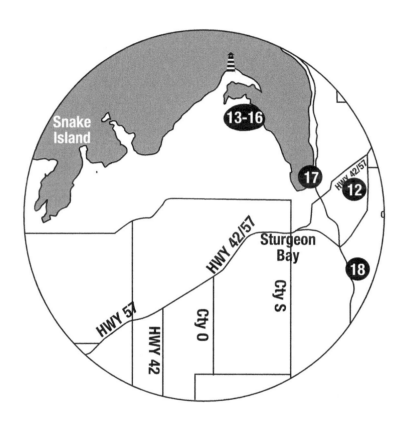

12. Crossroads at Big Creek Preserve
13. Potawatomi State Park - Ancient Shores Trail
14. Potawatomi State Park - Ice Age National Scenic Trail
15. Potawatomi State Park - Hemlock Trail
16. Potawatomi State Park - Tower Trail
17. Sunset Park
18. Franke Park

CHAPTER 3.

STURGEON BAY AREA

City of Sturgeon Bay, Little Sturgeon Bay and
Nasauwaupee Township

Sturgeon Bay is known to many visitors as the gateway to Door County, a place to pick up groceries, shop, or sightsee before heading to points further north. However, this vibrant little city is a great base for outdoor recreation. City parks offer surprisingly good wildlife watching opportunities; the harbor teams with birdlife, and it is the gateway to Potawatomi State Park, one of Wisconsin's best-loved state parks.

Originally home to bands of Menomonie and Chippewa, in the 1670s, Sturgeon Bay became a stop-off point on the Great Lakes for French-Canadian fur trappers and traders. Increase and Mary Claflin are generally credited as the first white settlers in Door County—they set up a residence near Little Sturgeon Bay around 1835, but after ten years of conflicts with local tribes, they moved on to Fish Creek. Other settlers came shortly thereafter including Peter Sherwood, who settled nearby on what is now Sherwood Point and Peter Rowley, the namesake of Rowleys Bay, who settled at the mouth of Sturgeon Bay. Later waves of immigrants from Norway, Germany, France, and England led to the extirpation of the last tribes from the area.

By the mid-1800s, Sturgeon Bay was booming as a center along the Great Lakes for logging, quarrying, shipbuilding, trapping, and trading. Completion of the Sturgeon Bay Ship Canal, in 1881, which provided a route around Death's Door passage, firmly established Sturgeon Bay as the main commercial hub for the region.

Today, with a year-round population of about 10,000, Sturgeon Bay continues its maritime tradition as a port and center for shipbuilding and remains the major commercial center for Door County. Despite the city's small size, it has a number of cultural offerings, summer events, excellent local parks, a waterfront geared toward visiting boaters, and abundant outdoor opportunities.

This is a community that embraces its position on the water, and its residents continue to work to protect wildlife and the environmental quality in the Green Bay and Lake Michigan. In the summer you'll see squadrons of American White Pelicans soaring in formation as you travel across the Bay Bridge, testament to offshore islands that were created to protect their breeding areas. You'll also see Ring-billed Gulls and Caspian Terns fishing along the waterfront, which also benefit from these same preservation efforts. Water quality is also improving, and with it, providing important refuge for migrating waterfowl.

12. Crossroads at Big Creek Preserve

Located on the outskirts of urban Sturgeon Bay, Crossroads at Big Creek is a science, outdoors, and natural history center for all ages, offering classes and events throughout the year. The 115-acre center has about 5.0 miles of trails, which run through open fields of seasonal wildflower and native grassland meadows and orchards. Trails also wind through towering stands of Eastern White Cedar along the namesake Big Creek, which empties into Lake Michigan at the property's southern border. Look for White-tailed Deer, Coyote, Racoon, Eastern Towhee, Song Sparrow, Tree Swallow, and Common Yellowthroat.

Paths are generally wide and mowed in the meadow areas, with some boardwalks. Note that the property has lots of seasonal wetlands and can be muddy, particularly in the spring and after a rainfall. From the Visitor Center parking lot, you can pick up the main trailhead. Trails are easy, well-marked, and you can generally see what's around the next bend, making it hard to get lost.

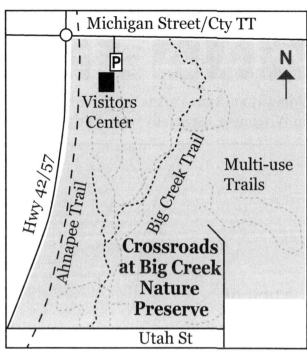

Mountain bikes are allowed on the trails, and if you are hiking, watch out for mountain bikers who might come around corners unexpectedly. In the winter, this spot is popular for snowshoeing and cross-country skiing, with rentals available at the Visitor Center during the winter season.

Trails, Access & Facilities: From the parking area, pick up the trailhead for 5.0 miles of trails.

Contact & Directions: Crossroads Preserve at Big Creek, www.crossroadsatbigcreek.org 2041 Michigan St., Sturgeon Bay, WI 54235. No Fee.

Potawatomi State Park is one of the most popular state parks in Wisconsin, especially with visiting families enjoying the

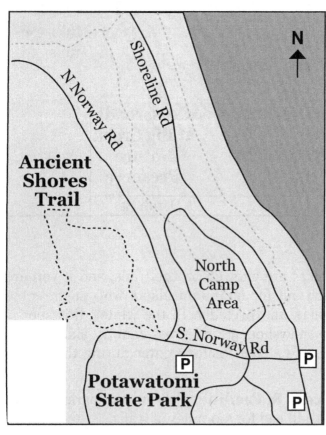

park's Visitor Center, kid-friendly beaches, and campgrounds. If you're looking for a short, easy interpretive trail, with lake views that is great for the kids, check out Ancient Shores Trail. This 0.5-mile interpretive loop trail winds through the namesake ancient shorelines of the area—you can see the rise and fall of Lake Michigan in geologic time.

Pick up the trailhead from the parking lot directly across from the Nature Center. While you're walking through Northern Mesic Forest community, dominated by Sugar Maple and American Beech, look for White-tailed Deer,

Red Fox, and Raccoon, and listen for American Redstart, Black-and-White Warbler, and Ovenbirds singing on territories in the summer months.

This trail is generally easy, quick, and kid-friendly, with few people.

Trails, Access & Facilities: Pick up the trailhead from the parking lot directly across from the Nature Center, and follow the 0.5-mile loop, which will return you to the parking area. There are restrooms in this area.

Contact: Wisconsin Department of Natural Resources, http://www.dnr.state.wi.us/. The main entrance is at 3740 County PD, Sturgeon Bay, WI 54235.

14. Potawatomi State Park – Ice Age National Scenic Trail

With over 1,200 acres, Potawatomi State Park is one of Wisconsin's favorite state parks, and on summer days it can feel a bit crowded. If you're looking for a break from the crowds and a more challenging hike, look no further than hiking a stretch of one of the premier trails in all of Wisconsin, the Ice Age National Scenic Trail. The Ice Age National Scenic Trail is one of Wisconsin's longest trails, stretching more than 1,200 miles across the state. The trail starts (or ends) here at Potawatomi State Park.

This first (or last) portion of the Ice Age National Scenic Trail runs 2.8 miles along a glaciated ridge on the park's eastern edge and then continues outside the park's boundaries to the south. It is especially recommended for those interested in getting a bit more off the beaten path.

You'll climb moderate bluffs along the Lake Michigan shoreline, tracing the trail of the ancient glaciers through

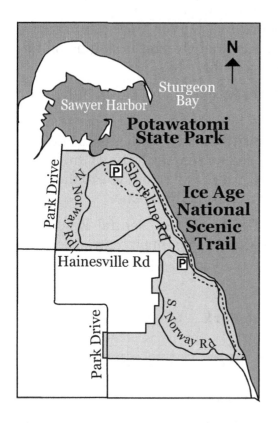

old Eastern White Cedar, Sugar Maple and American Beech. Along the lakeshore, the trail traverses past a Moist Cliff community comprised of Northern Wet Mesic Forest with a well-developed native fern understory on the bluffs. In the interior Northern Hardwood, Northern Mesic, and Northern Wet Mesic forests, look for nesting Rose-breasted Grosbeak, Pileated Woodpecker, Black-throated Green Warbler, and Wood Thrush, as well as Raccoons, Gray Squirrel, White-tailed Deer, Striped Skunk, and Meadow Vole.

From the Old Ski Hill Overlook parking area, drop your car and head east along the park's main road for about 0.2 miles to the trailhead. You'll head up and down the bluffs for about 0.4 miles. Watch out for slips and slides, as this trail may be steep and muddy in places. You'll then cross the park road and follow the trail south along the Lake Michigan bluffs for about 2.2 miles to the park's southern border. Retrace your steps back along the bluffs to return to your car. This trail not only has great views but is probably the most challenging in all of Door County.

Trails, Access & Facilities: Park at the Old Ski Hill Overlook parking lot at the observation tower. This area has rest rooms.

Contact: Wisconsin Department of Natural Resources, http://www.dnr.state.wi.us/. The main entrance is at 3740 County PD, Sturgeon Bay, WI 54235. Fee area.

15. Potawatomi State Park – Hemlock Trail

Potawatomi State Park, a popular 1,200-acre state park with its steep ravines, rocky beaches, and towering limestone cliffs along the Sturgeon Bay, provides year-round wildlife viewing, hiking, camping, and boating opportunities. The Hemlock Trail traverses 2.6 miles along the Green Bay shoreline and inland, and is one of the park's most popular hikes.

From Parking Lot 2, you'll follow the red-blazed trail north along the lake over the bluffs for about 0.5 miles, where

65

it runs along with the Tower Trail. During the summer, peek through the Eastern White Cedar forests along the 150-foot bluffs in this stretch to look for Caspian Terns, gulls, American White Pelicans, and Double-crested Cormorants flying past along the lake.

The trail then breaks off from the Tower Trail and starts heading inland. Continue here for about another 0.5 miles past the southern end of the campground and the Nature Center. Cross the park road and then turn due south for about 1.0 miles through Northern Mesic forests. In the forests, listen for Hermit Thrush, American Robin, Black-capped Chickadee, and Ovenbird.

The trail will then head due east, and you'll again cross the main park road and follow along past the group campground. This area is more open, and you can watch for Indigo Bunting, Eastern Kingbird, and American Goldfinch in the scrubby field edges. Follow this for another 0.6 miles back to the parking area where you started.

During the summer, this trail can be popular in spots, particularly where it leads through some of the campground areas. In the off-season, you'll have the place to yourself.

Trails, Access & Facilities: Pick up the Hemlock Trail trailhead at Parking Lot 2 near the picnic area, which has bathrooms with running water. You'll never be more than 0.5 miles from the park road if you need facilities, and it's tough to truly get lost.

Contact: Wisconsin Department of Natural Resources, http://www.dnr.state.wi.us/. The main entrance is at 3740 County PD, Sturgeon Bay, WI 54235. Fee area.

16. Potawatomi State Park - Tower Trail

Today it's hard to picture Door County as a downhill skiing destination, but Peninsula State Park's Tower Trail sits atop a historic ski hill. Hike up to the top of the bluff along the shores of Lake Michigan on a bluebird summer day or in the fall when the leaves are turning, with views of the harbors and boats below, and you'll truly understand what all the fuss is about. At the top, you'll be at one of the highest points for miles and on clear days can see all the way to Chambers Island and across to Michigan's Upper Peninsula.

For almost 100 years, visitors to Potawatomi State Park have hiked up to Wisconsin's most famous points on the Tower Trail, a 3.6 mile trail across the Niagara Escarpment and bluffs over Green Bay.

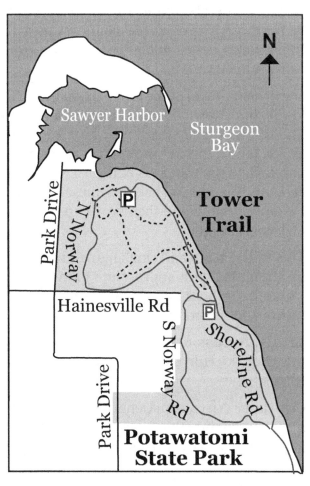

The park's vistas provide an excellent vantage point for watching and listening for spring migrant and breeding warblers and watching for migrating raptors. The area also provides panoramic views of Green Bay.

If you're not feeling up to the trail, you can park in the lot near Old Ski Hill Overlook and enjoy the views near the parking.

For the whole 3.6 mile loop, while you can start at the Old Ski Hill Overlook parking at the tower, we like to start at the lot along Shoreline Road to pick up the trail along the lake first and head north for about 0.7 mile to the site of the old observation tower. This stretch of trail is generally easy to moderate, but it climbs up the bluffs and may not be for those who don't feel comfortable with heights. The trail quickly bends inland to the tower, where you'll start gaining in elevation.

Once you've tackled the hill, pick up the trail again and follow it south down the old ski hill area for about 0.75 miles. The trail gradually turns east back towards the lake, and as you follow this for another 0.5 miles, you will come to a point when the trail goes both east and south. You can cut across east and head back to your car or go south through the campground and then north up the lakeshore for a bit of extra mileage.

This trail is steep and challenging in spots and should only be attempted with appropriate footwear. It's also a great workout for those interested in trail running, though be on the lookout for roots and rocks.

Trails, Access & Facilities: Pick up the trailhead from the Old Ski Hill Overlook parking. This area has rest rooms.

Contact: Wisconsin Department of Natural Resources, http://www.dnr.state.wi.us/. The main entrance is at 3740 County PD, Sturgeon Bay, WI 54235. Fee area.

17. Sunset Park

Sunset Park packs a lot of activity into just 41 acres. This urban park includes a small freshwater lake, Bradley Lake, and excellent views of the Sturgeon Bay on the Green Bay side of the Peninsula. The park has amenities, including a public access dock and boat ramps, Frisbee golf course, kids' playground areas, basketball and tennis courts, a sheltered swimming beach, and a picnic pavilion, along with 0.5 miles of paved trails.

This park is also popular for fishing, boating, dog walking, jogging, swimming, and other recreation, and you can also put in canoes, standup paddleboard, and kayaks at one of two ramps to access the Sturgeon Bay. It is also a good spot to bring the kids, have a picnic, swim in the lake, or watch the sunset. Given the park's popularity with families, runners, walkers, and boaters—locals and tourists alike, out enjoying the fine views of Sturgeon Bay, during the busy season, visits in the early morning are recommended if you want to avoid the crowds.

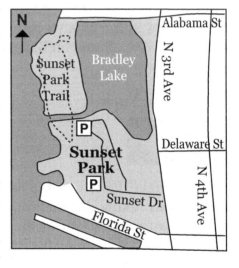

Despite its urban setting and heavy foot traffic, Sunset Park can be surprisingly good for wildlife watching. In the warmer months, look around the lake edges for Black-crowned Night Heron, Green Heron, and Common Yellowthroat. The park also provides an excellent vantage point to watch for White Pelicans, Herring Gull, Caspian

Tern, Ring-billed Gull, and Double-crested Cormorants, all of which breed in local colonies on offshore islands of the Green Bay. This area can also be an excellent spot during spring and fall migration for migrating raptors and songbirds. During the fall, winter, and spring, Bradley Lake can be good for a diversity of waterfowl, especially large flocks of Canada Geese.

Trails, Access & Facilities: The park has a number of walking paths, public access dock and boat ramps, Frisbee golf course, kids' playground areas, basketball and tennis courts, a sheltered swimming beach, picnic area, and rest rooms.

Contact: City of Sturgeon Bay Parks and Recreation, http://www.sturgeonbaywi.org. Sunset Park is located at 747 N. 3rd Ave., Sturgeon Bay, WI, 54235. No fee.

18. Franke Park

While Franke Park won't hold any special appeal as a world-class hiking destination, this is a perfect place for a quick jaunt to get out of the car after a long road trip or to take the kids for a short walk. This 6.5-acre City of Sturgeon Bay park, located south of Hwy 42 on Clay Banks Road, has a 0.5-mile loop trail, with a few boardwalks, through a Northern Wet Mesic White Cedar swamp, with small patches of Northern Hardwood Swamp and Northern Sedge Meadow wetlands.

This park is urban and is primarily used by neighborhood residents for dog walking or pushing a stroller. It's an excellent choice for those who can't walk very far or are walking with small children but still want to enjoy being in a wooded area. However, you'll want to remember to bring your bug spray! The urban park has many of the common woodland birds and animals, including Racoon, Red Squirrel, Blue Jay, Black-capped Chickadee, and Cedar Waxwing.

Trails, Access & Facilities: There are no facilities.

Contact: City of Sturgeon Bay Parks and Recreation, http://www.sturgeon-baywi.org. 1700 Clay Banks Rd., Sturgeon Bay, WI 54235. No fee.

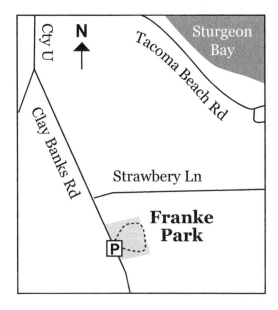

EGG HARBOR AND FISH CREEK AREA

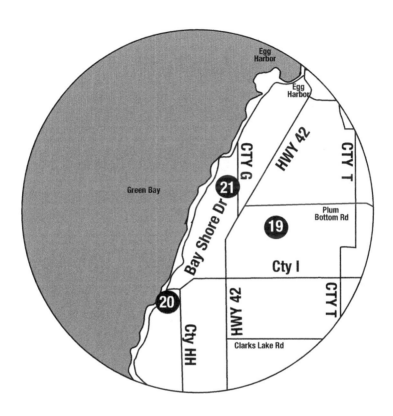

19. Oak Road Wetlands Preserve

20. Bay Shore Bluffland Preserve & State Natural Area

21. Lautenback Woods Preserve

CHAPTER 4.

EGG HARBOR AND FISH CREEK AREA

Egg Harbor, Fish Creek, Sevastopol
Township, and Carlsville

Popular with tourists and travelers for more than 150 years, the settlements of Egg Harbor and Fish Creek, located along the shores of the Green Bay, provide some of the most scenic vistas in all of Door County. Along Lake Michigan, you'll find picturesque harbors, warm(er!) water beaches, and towering forests growing out of the rocky bluffs along the Niagara Escarpment. Inland, family farms and cherry orchards dot the landscape.

In the late 1800s, Asa Thorp built the first permanent settlement in the area, and the harbor communities known as Fish Creek and Egg Harbor quickly grew, first attracting English settlers, who were soon followed by French-Canadian fur traders, trappers, and farmers from Germany and Scandinavia. The Thorp family built busy docks at both Fish Creek and Egg Harbor, spurring on a logging, farming, fishing, and trading boom in the area.

Resort development soon followed, with the summer communities drawing tourists from St. Louis, Chicago, and Milwaukee, many of whom built their own summer homes along the lakeshore in the early 1900s. Today, little has changed. The beaches, small town charm, outdoor opportunities, towering bluffs, and lake breezes of Fish Creek and Egg Harbor continue to draw summer visitors from all over the world to this part of Door County.

19. Oak Road Wetlands Preserve

The 155-acre Oak Road Wetlands Preserve, managed by the Door County Land Trust, includes native prairie restoration along Oak Road and Sunnyslope Road, just south of Egg Harbor, and protects the headwaters of the West Branch of the Whitefish Bay Creek.

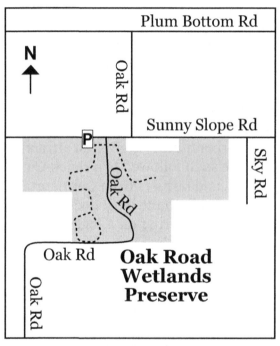

There are 1.75 miles of flat, easy hiking trails on the preserve itself, but the preserve is also easily viewed by pulling off to the side of the road for those with less mobility. Birding and wildlife viewing are the primary attractions, and you can walk the relatively flat trails through restored native prairie and wildflower meadows, bustling with birds and butterflies in the summer months, to a viewing platform that overlooks the wetlands. In the winter you can snowshoe the same trails. This is also a nice starting point for a bike ride in the Egg Harbor area, up and down rolling hills and past bucolic farms and orchards. Fall colors in this area can be spectacular.

In addition to the native prairie restoration, Oak Road

Wetlands is best known for its ephemeral, or seasonal, wetlands that flood with the spring rains. When the wetlands get rain, the abundant Eastern Spring Peepers can seemingly be heard for miles, giving rise to the local nickname for this spot—Frog Town. Where water conditions are right, these wetlands provide important habitat for amphibians and migrant shorebirds like Wilson's Phalarope, Dunlin, and Short-billed Dowitcher, which breed in the Canadian Arctic and Prairie Pothole regions and winter along the Gulf Coast and points south. In the summer and fall, in the drier upland prairie areas, look for grassland specialist birds like Savannah, Vesper and Clay-colored Sparrows, Sandhill Crane, Bobolink, Eastern Kingbird, and Eastern Meadowlark. The Door County Land Trust has also installed nest boxes used by Eastern Bluebirds and Tree Swallows.

Trails, Access & Facilities: Pick up the 1.75-mile loop trail from the parking lot. Hunting and leashed dogs are authorized pursuant to DCLT guidelines and permission. There are no facilities.

Contact & Directions: Door County Land Trust, http://www.doorcountylandtrust.org/. 6391 Oak Rd., Egg Harbor, WI 54209. No fee.

20. Bay Shore Blufflands Preserve/Bay Shore Blufflands State Natural Area

The Bay Shore Blufflands Preserve, protected by private landowners, the Door County Land Trust, and the Nature Conservancy, traverses some of the tallest bluffs in Door County, some rising up to 200 feet above the Green Bay shoreline. Hands down, this preserve offers some of the best hiking in Door County and is one of our favorite trails out-

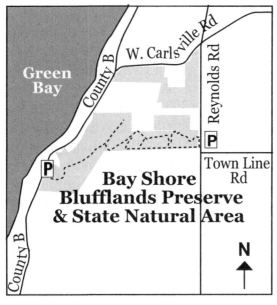

Green Bay

W. Carlsville Rd

Reynolds Rd

County B

County B

Town Line Rd

Bay Shore Blufflands Preserve & State Natural Area

N ↑

side of the state parks. The Door County Land Trust maintains about 2.5 miles of hiking trails on a 150-acre parcel roughly bounded by Reynolds Road and Bay Shore Drive.

This area includes a three-mile long stretch of the Niagara Escarpment and a number of distinct ecological communities. The bluffs of the Niagara Escarpment form microclimate that supports pockets of rare Moist Cliff Community, characterized by native ferns and Wild Sarsaparilla. This preserve also has massive ancient Eastern White Cedars typical of the surrounding Northern Wet Mesic Forest community and other hardwood trees typical of the surrounding Northern Mesic Forest community. There are seeps and ephemeral springs and wetlands that flood annually below and near the bottom of the Escarpment, supporting a very unique Clay Seepage Bluff community along with wetter pockets of Northern Hardwood Swamp including Silver Maple, Green Ash, and Swamp White Oak.

Along Green Bay, you'll find a small wetlands area with Northern Sedge Meadow and Emergent Marsh communities and an ephemeral creek. Near the top of the Escarpment, a Northern Mesic Forest community gradually gives way to a drier pine-dominated Northern Dry Mesic Forest, with an understory of ferns, Goldenrod, and Dogwood. This can be an exceptional place to look for spring wildflowers including orchids. Bayshore Blufflands Preserve also supports a community of rare understory plants and animals including Dwarf Lake Iris, Canada Yew, and Northern Ring-necked Snake.

Trails, Access & Facilities: There are 2.5 miles of hiking trails on the Door County Land Trust parcels, generally hiked as an out and back trail. There are also a few side loops if you want to take a shorter path. There are two trailheads one on each side of the preserve. The trail can be completed by parking your car at either the east or west trailhead and retracing your steps to return or leaving a car at each side and completing a through-hike from end to end. Trails are moderate, but may be steep or rocky along the escarpment, and should be reserved for those with appropriate footwear. Leashed dogs are permitted. Bikes, horses, and motorized vehicles are prohibited. Hunting is authorized pursuant to DCLT guidelines and permission.

Contact & Directions: Door County Land Trust, http://www.doorcountylandtrust.org/. The Nature Conservancy, http://www.nature.org. The trailheads are located at 5454 Bay Shore Dr. (County B), Sturgeon Bay, WI 54235, and 5519 Reynolds Rd., Sturgeon Bay, WI 54235. The trail runs between these two parking areas. No fee.

21. Lautenbach Woods Preserve

If you're looking for a place to get up close and personal with the Niagara Escarpment, the Lautenbach Woods Preserve is an excellent place to do it. Lautenbach Woods is an 80-acre parcel owned and managed by the Door County Land Trust. Not only is this site beautiful, it also provides important protection of local watersheds (in other words, the underground water reserves that feed local wetlands

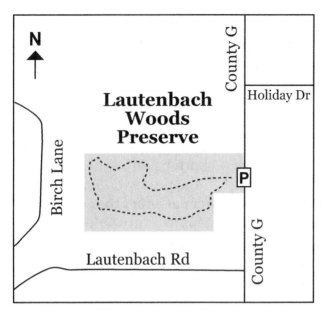

and creeks).

This area is best known for its karst features and caves, and this site has a well-maintained, moderate loop hiking trail of about 1.25 miles which gives you access to some of those areas. The site contains one of the largest cave systems in northeastern Wisconsin, associated with the Niagara Escarpment, and the Door County Land Trust occasionally offers tours to see some of these karst areas.

With or without a tour, this makes a great hike and is one of the more challenging hikes in the area. Along the trail, you'll stroll through scenic forests and wetlands and traverse some rocky outcrops as you head up along the Niagara Escarpment. Trails are moderate overall, but can be challenging in some places, with tree roots and slick spots, and sturdy footwear is highly recommended.

Lautenbach Woods Preserve is predominantly Northern Mesic Forest community, with a substantial component of really big, old White Pine and Eastern Hemlock, as well as pockets of Northern Hardwood Swamp community and some ephemeral wetlands that flood with the spring rains. From the trails, hikers can explore Niagara Escarpment outcrops and listen for Hermit Thrush, Indigo Bunting, American Redstart, Red-breasted Nuthatch, Black-capped Chickadee, and Least Flycatcher. At dusk, keep an eye out for Big Brown and Red Bats.

Trails, Access & Facilities: The preserve contains a well-maintained, 1.25-mile loop trail. The trail is moderate overall but is steep and rocky in some areas. There are no facilities. Leashed dogs are permitted. Bikes, horses, and motorized vehicles are prohibited. Hunting is authorized pursuant to DCLT guidelines and permission.

Contact: Door County Land Trust, http://www.door-countylandtrust.org/. A small parking lot with picnic tables is located on the west side of County G at 6749 County Rd. G, Egg Harbor, WI 54209. No fee.

KANGAROO LAKE TO WHITEFISH DUNES

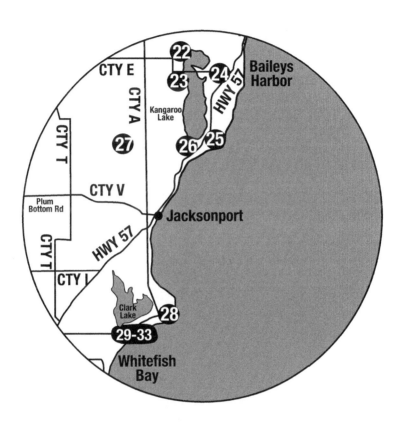

22. **Kangaroo Lake Preserve**

23. **Kangaroo Lake-TNC Trail**

24. **Kangaroo Lake-Door County Land Trust Trail**

25. **Heins Creek Nature Preserve**

26. **Meridian County Park & Lyle Harter-Matter Sanctuary**

27. **Hibbard's Creek Natural Area**

28. **Cave Point County Park**

29-33. **Whitefish Dunes State Park**

CHAPTER 5.

KANGAROO LAKE TO WHITEFISH DUNES

Jacksonport, Valmy, and Sevastopol Township

The stretch from Kangaroo Lake to Whitefish Dunes State Park is indelibly marked by the ancient glaciers that covered this part of Door County 5,000 to 10,000 years ago. When you look at the massive sand dunes left behind, separating Clark Lake and Kangaroo Lake from Lake Michigan, it's easy to imagine a time when the last of the glaciers receded. After the glaciers, 1,000 years ago, these woods around Kangaroo Lake and Whitefish Dunes were home to native tribes, who fished and foraged around these waters.

The first European settlers arrived in the early to mid-1800s, clearing lands around Kangaroo Lake for farming, and building sawmills, shipping docks, and infrastructure along the Whitefish Dunes. This area prospered as a commercial center for fishing, logging, shipping, and trading through the late 1880s. By the late 1880s, the area began to transition into a summer resort community, which drew visitors from Milwaukee, Chicago, and beyond. Many stayed to build cottages along the lakeshores, a tradition that continues to this day.

Today, Kangaroo Lake's popularity with boaters, sailors, and anglers in search of panfish, bass, and walleye continues, while Clark Lake provides a quieter, more relaxing setting. This part of Door County, known as "the quiet side," is a perfect alternative to the summer tourist traffic and busy downtowns along the other side of the peninsula.

22. Kangaroo Lake – Kangaroo Lake Preserve (Northwest Side of Kangaroo Lake)

From above, the shape of this glacial lake is said to resemble the Australian animal, and local cottage owners will refer to their location on the lake at the ears, the tail, or the pouch of the kangaroo. Kangaroo Lake is lined with private cottages and resorts but maintains its quiet character, thanks in part to the protection of several large parcels owned by the Nature Conservancy and the Door County Land Trust. These well-maintained and extremely scenic hiking trails are popular with the lake's summer residents. Though very few visitors know about this corner of Kangaroo Lake, we consider it to be some of the most beautiful hiking in all of Door County.

One of the best ways to access Kangaroo Lake itself is through this trail through about 250 acres of pristine wetlands owned by the Door County Land Trust. There is no

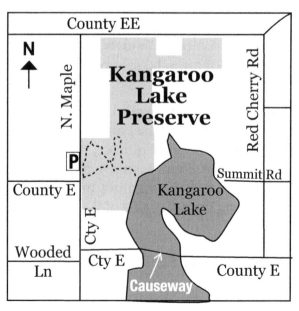

parking lot, but you can pull off the east side of Maple Road. The trail is moderate, starting at one of the higher points in the area, and traverses down through an open Northern Mesic Forest, along outcrops of the Niagara Escarpments, past old stone walls from the preserve's agricultural past, and down to an extensive cattail marsh along the lakeshore. This trail is about 1.5 miles roundtrip and is relatively steep and can be slippery in some areas. The lake views and sense of solitude in nature are unparalleled.

Watch for wildlife like Muskrat, Sandhill Crane, Beaver, Hine's Emerald Dragonfly, Eastern Peeper, Common Goldeneye, Osprey, Black Tern, Caspian Tern, and Bald Eagle along the lakeshores and wetlands.

Trails, Access & Facilities: The trail is about 1.5 miles roundtrip and is relatively steep in some areas. Marked trails from trailheads are well developed, and both the DCLT and TNC parcels on the northwest side of the lake have excellent trail networks and can be accessed from the trailhead on the east side of N Maple Road or the TNC parking lot on County E. This trail includes access to the lake, and wetlands along Piel Creek. Leashed dogs are permitted. Bikes, horses, and motorized vehicles are prohibited on the DCLT preserve. Hunting is authorized on DCLT parcels pursuant to DCLT guidelines and permission.

Contact: Door County Land Trust, http://www.doorcountylandtrust.org/. Park off the shoulder of N. Maple Rd. at 7912 N. Maple Rd., Baileys Harbor, WI 54202, and head east from the trailhead. No fee.

23. Kangaroo Lake - TNC Trail (West Side of Kangaroo Lake)

Flowing into Kangaroo Lake, Peil Creek feeds Northern Sedge Meadow and Emergent Marshes, forming a large wetlands complex along the spring-fed headwaters of the

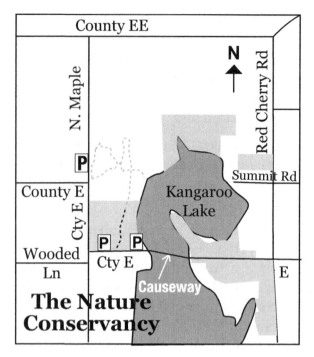

lake. These wetlands are synonymous with the Hine's Emerald Dragonfly. This area represents the core breeding habitat for the endangered dragonfly. Look for Water Lilly, Cattails, and Bulrush in the shallower parts of the lake. Careful observers may also find Beaver, Muskrat, Northern Leopard Frog, Wood Frog, Dorcas Copper Butterfly, Sandhill Crane, Common Goldeneye, Osprey, Black Tern, and Bald Eagle along the lakeshores and wetlands.

Inland, the northern and western shore of Kangaroo Lake includes pockets of Northern Wet Mesic Forest with a diverse understory, including plants such as Canada Yew and a well-developed Willow-Alder community. A causeway, today part of County E, was built in the 1800s and bisects the northern and southern parts of the lake. The causeway also provides easy access for those who only have a few minutes to stop and look at the lake.

The Nature Conservancy manages a well-maintained trail along Piel Creek which links to the Door County Land Trust trail near the lake. The trail begins at a parking lot located at 3090 County E. This parking lot is located just south of the Door County Land Trust trail parking. The TNC trail is about 1.0 miles roundtrip and meanders through similar habitat, ending at the same cattail marsh along Kangaroo Lake. This trail provides excellent views of the lake.

Trails, Access & Facilities: The trails on the TNC property are about 1.0 miles total, linking up with the DCLT trails. Marked trails from trailheads on the DCLT and TNC properties on are well developed. Both the DCLT and TNC parcels on the northwest side of the lake have excellent trail networks and can be accessed from the trailhead on the east side of N Maple Road or the TNC parking lot on County E. Both trailheads link to about 1.5 miles of hiking trails, including access to the lake, and wetlands along Piel Creek. The TNC site is subject to TNC access rules and posted hours. There is parking for several cars, a kiosk, and trail signage at the County E trailhead.

Contact & Directions: The Nature Conservancy, http://www.nature.org. Trailhead parking is located at 3090 County E, Baileys Harbor, WI 54202. No fee.

24. Kangaroo Lake - Door County Land Trust Trail (East Side of Kangaroo Lake)

On the eastern side of Kangaroo Lake, across the causeway, the Door County Land Trust owns additional land which is also open to the public. The approximately 1.0 mile of trail in this area is less developed, tend to be infrequently used, and a bit overgrown.

The trail traverses through Eastern White Cedar swamps and wetlands at the "mouth" and "chin" of the Kangaroo. Appropriate footwear is essential, as is a willingness to traverse sometimes overgrown trails. You're guaranteed to have the place to yourself, and might see wildlife like Beaver, Hine's Emerald Dragonfly, Muskrat, Sandhill Crane,

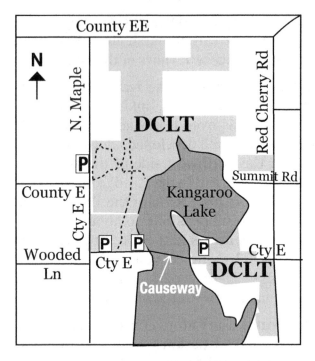

Eastern Peeper, Common Goldeneye, Osprey, Caspian Tern, and Bald Eagle along the lakeshores and wetlands.

Pack your bug spray, shoes that can get wet, and a healthy sense of adventure if you plan to take on these trails.

Contact & Directions: Door County Land Trust, http://www.doorcountylandtrust.org/. The trailhead is on the eastern side of the Kangaroo Lake causeway around 2829 County Rd. E, Baileys Harbor, WI 54202. Look for a pull out and DCLT sign just east and across the road from the clock shop. The trails can be reached by parking off the north side of County E about 0.1 mile east of the eastern end of the causeway.

25. Kangaroo Lake - Heins Creek Nature Preserve (South Side of Kangaroo Lake)

Heins Creek is one of the small streams and wetlands that flows into Kangaroo Lake. Situated along the southern shores of Kangaroo Lake, adjacent to Meridian County Park, this 75-acre preserve, protected by the Door County Land Trust, has about 0.75 miles of hiking trails. This area is an example of the changing landscapes of the

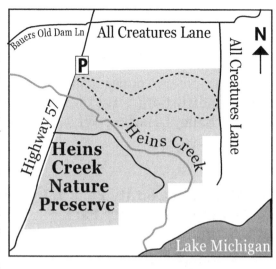

Door Peninsula in the last 5,000 years. Glaciers shaped this region, leaving sand dunes that separated Kangaroo Lake from Lake Michigan. Following the glaciers, Native Americans settled the area and fished for trout and salmon along Heins Creek and Kangaroo Lake. Archeological digs in this area reveal that the site was once home to settlements of the North Bay, Late Woodland, and Oneota peoples more than 1,000 years ago.

Today, the Heins Creek area forms an isthmus between Lake Michigan and Kangaroo Lake, complete with massive ancient sand dunes, now covered in Northern Wet Mesic and upland Northern Hardwood forests and a diverse understory of ferns. In the summer, large Eastern White Cedar, Eastern Hemlock, and White Birch groves are punctuated by the calls of Ovenbirds, and along the wetlands, you might see Muskrat and waterfowl like Common Goldeneye and Common Merganser. In the spring and fall look for spawning fish.

Trails, Access & Facilities: The trail is a 0.75-mile loop trail accessible from Highway 57 and can be muddy in areas. Leashed dogs are permitted. Bikes, horses, and motorized vehicles are prohibited on the DCLT preserve.

Hunting is authorized on DCLT parcels pursuant to DCLT guidelines and permission. Use caution along Highway 57, as traffic can move fast.

Contact: Door County Land Trust, http://www.door-countylandtrust.org/. Park off the shoulder at 7112 Highway 57, Baileys Harbor, WI 54202, and head north the trailhead. No fee.

26. Meridian County Park & Lyle-Harter-Matter Sanctuary County Park

Named for its geographic location at the 45th parallel, halfway between the North Pole and the Equator, Meridian County Park and the Lyle-Harter-Matter Sanctuary protect a complex of lands on the southern shore of Kangaroo Lake along Highway 57. Over the years, The Nature Conservancy, Door County Land Trust, local landowner families, and others have bought up a number of adjacent parcels, and, along with the Heins Creek Preserve, protect the headwaters of Heins Creek, which flows into Kangaroo Lake. Despite the various names, this area is now a contiguous unit and is designated as a State Natural Area.

The park is very scenic, although you might hear some road noise from Hwy 57. Trails are not well developed or well-marked, but the area is small enough to prevent visitors from truly getting lost. This park is also popular for mountain biking.

The area is well wooded, with Northern Wet Mesic forests growing atop an ancient Great Lakes Beach and Dune community, and well-worn glacial Great Lakes Ridge and Swale along the isthmus between Lake Michigan and the south end of Kangaroo Lake. The area is dominated by a Northern Mesic Forest with some Northern Wet Mesic Forest, with substantial stands of American Beech. Prior to overgrazing by White-tailed Deer, the park had a well-developed understory of Wood Fern, Canada Yew, and Canada Mayflower, but now many of the

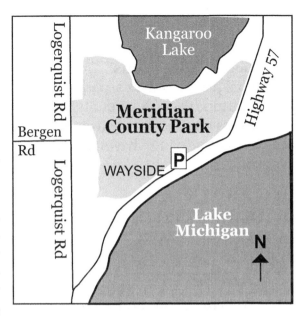

plants along the forest floor are gone. This has effectively eliminated the presence of understory-nesting birds like Black-throated Blue Warbler, former local breeders in the park.

The original Meridian County Park section is also noteworthy for its Clay Seepage Bluff communities-damp, mossy, and dramatic 15-foot dolomite rock outcrops, characteristic of the Niagara Escarpment, which provide habitat for a variety of plants and animals, including Wood Frog, Blue-spotted Salamander, and Northern Waterthrush. Some sections include several areas of Emergent Marsh, the springs that feed Kangaroo Lake, and 60-foot forested ancient sand dunes.

Trails, Access & Facilities: The best trail access into the park is at the Hwy 57 rest stop wayside located at 6799 Hwy 57 between Jacksonport and Baileys Harbor. The easiest way to access the trails is to park at the wayside and follow the path behind the restrooms. Restrooms and parking are located at the wayside, but the site is otherwise undeveloped. There is no trail signage, and trails are not well-marked, but are easy to follow. There are several miles of trails throughout the property beginning behind the restrooms.

Contact & Directions: Door County Parks System, http://map.co.door.wi.us/parks/. Door County Land Trust, http://www.doorcountylandtrust.org/. The best trail access into the park is from the Hwy 57 rest stop wayside located at 6799 Hwy 57, Baileys Harbor, WI 54202. No fee.

27. Hibbard's Creek Natural Area

This 80-acre parcel, protected by the Door County Land Trust, includes a significant wetlands complex along Hibbard's Creek. The preserve has about 0.5 miles roundtrip of rustic trails, which are not well-marked and may not always be well maintained, but get some foot traffic from anglers. In addition, from Junction Road, where the road crosses Hibbard Creek, there are stairs and a wooden platform. This platform provides views of the creek on both sides of the road and is designed for launching canoes and kayaks and for wading access for fishing.

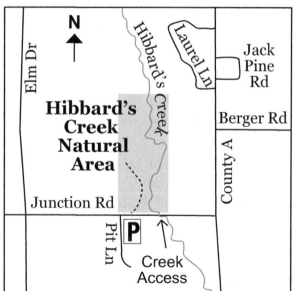

Hibbard's Creek is a

well-known trout stream, stocked annually by the Wisconsin Department of Natural Resources with Rainbow Trout, Brook Trout, and Steelhead. The preserve includes a number of Emergent Marsh areas and springs and is home to Red-winged Blackbird, Song Sparrow, and Muskrat. In addition to wetlands, the preserve includes Northern Wet Mesic and Northern Dry Mesic Forest communities, with breeding Rose-breasted Grosbeak, American Robin, Eastern Kingbird, Scarlett Tanager, and Red-eyed Vireo. In addition to fish habitat, the preserve provides habitat for a variety of riparian plants including Marsh Horsetail and Slender Bog-Arrowgrass.

Trails, Access & Facilities: The preserve contains a rustic, occasionally maintained trail of about 0.25 miles to the wetlands area near the creek. The trail begins at the border of the property with the neighboring farm field and ends at the creek. Areas near the creek may be wet, and visitors should wear appropriate footwear or waders if fishing. There are no facilities. Leashed dogs are permitted. Bikes, horses, and motorized vehicles are prohibited. Hunting is authorized pursuant to DCLT guidelines and permission.

Contact & Directions: Door County Land Trust, http://www.doorcountylandtrust.org/. The trailhead can be accessed from N. Junction Rd. just east of the intersection with Pit Ln. Park off the shoulder of N. Junction Rd. just past the intersection at about 3548 Junction Rd. Egg Harbor, WI 54209. Proceed northeast on foot to the trailhead. You can see the wooded platform for fishing and boat launching where Junction Rd. crosses the creek. No fee.

28. Cave Point County Park

Cave Point County Park, owned and operated by the Door County Parks System, is one of the most popular spots

in Door County for swimming, kayaking, cave exploration, picnicking, and hiking atop the bluffs. The park includes several underwater caves, limestone bluffs, and sweeping views of Lake Michigan, and is well worth a visit for the scenic Lake Michigan overlooks alone. Surrounded on three sides by Whitefish Dunes State Park, Cave Point provides hiking access to the state park via an easy loop hiking trail.

Caution is due here. While the caves are cool, and jumping off the bluffs is a big draw, this area has claimed the lives of swimmers and paddlers in recent years. Crumbling trails along the bluffs are also a hazard.

The main trail is referred to on maps as the Cave Point Lakeside Trail, which runs along Lake Michigan for about 1.2 miles, give or take, and links up with trails at Whitefish Dunes. While you're on the trails, it is tough to tell where the county park ends and the state park begins, and this trail can easily be combined with the trails at Whitefish. The Lakeside trail passes through Northern Wet Mesic Forest. Inland, look for Northern Mesic Forests, with well-developed native fern understory.

This area can also be a good place to look for Wood Frog, Red-backed Salamander, and Spotted Salamander. Cave Point County Park is an excellent spot to find breeding Mourning Warbler, particularly in areas with extensive fern understory along the main road into the park. Chestnut-sided Warbler, Red-eyed Vireo, and Great-crested Flycatcher also breed here. In the winter, look for the tracks of Snowshoe Hare, Raccoon, Ermine, and Porcupine. The park is hugely popular in the summer months, often overrun with people, and even in the off-season is popular. While you'll never really have Cave Point all to yourself, it is iconic for a reason, and is a must-stop location in this part of Door County.

Trails, Access & Facilities: Cave Point County Park has about 1.2 miles of hiking trails that link up with hiking trails at Whitefish Dunes State Park, easily accessible from the parking lot. Cave Point also has an overlook for viewing several sections of an impressive underwater cave along the Lake Michigan shoreline, along with parking, restrooms, and a picnic area. Leashed dogs are allowed.

Contact & Directions: Door County Parks System, http://map.co.door.wi.us/parks/. Park entrance is located at 5360 Schauer Rd., Sturgeon Bay, WI 54235. No fee.

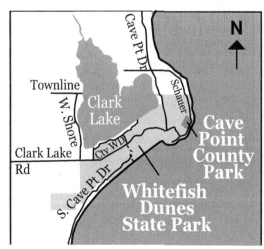

29. Whitefish Dunes State Park– Black Trail

Whitefish Dunes is a very popular park during the summer months, and with good reason. The 865-acre park has hiking and biking trails, a nature center, picnic areas, interpretive programs, archaeological sites, and, depending on lake levels, great beaches. Whitefish Dunes is home to the largest sand dunes on Lake Michigan, and its wide sandy beaches and the relatively shallow waters of Whitefish Bay make it an ideal swimming beach. Inland, the bike paths, picnic areas, and visitor center are also popular with vacationers.

The Black Trail, a 2.5-mile loop trail, is one of the park's better traveled routes and links up to the Lakeside Trail in Cave Point County Park. Pick up the trail at the main parking area, and follow the flat, relatively easy trail along the Lake Michigan shoreline before it bends inland. There are plenty of breaks in the trees for glimpses of the lake, and throughout you can hear the crashing waves of Lake Michigan. Inland, stands of dead trees, which struggle to find footing in this sandy and rocky soil, have been left intact. These standing 'snags' are fantastic for woodpeckers, and this is one of the few places left in the state where Red-headed Woodpeckers can be seen with some regularity. More common Downy, Hairy, Red-bellied, and Pileated Woodpeckers are also found here.

Trails, Access & Facilities: Pick up the 2.5-mile loop Black Trail from the main parking area. The park has parking, restrooms, and picnic areas. Leashed dogs are allowed.

Contact & Directions: Wisconsin Dept. Natural Resources, http://dnr.wi.gov. The park entrance is at 3275 Clark Lake Rd., Sturgeon Bay, WI 54235. Fee area.

30. Whitefish Dunes State Park—Brachiopod Trail

865-acre Whitefish Dunes State Park boasts hiking and biking trails, a nature center, picnic areas, interpretive programs, archaeological sites, and great beaches, making it a favorite for vacationers from all corners of the world. Whitefish Dunes is home to the largest sand dunes on Lake Michigan, and depending on lake levels, its wide sandy beaches and the relatively shallow waters of Whitefish Bay make it an ideal swimming beach. Inland, the bike paths, picnic areas, and visitor center are also popular.

Named after an ancient fossil found in Door County, the 1.5-mile connector and interpretive Brachiopod Trail is one of the park's easier tracks. The flat, generally easy trail has a series of interpretive signage explaining the fossil history, plants, and animals found in the park and is suitable for families and anyone who can walk on moderate surfaces over sand.

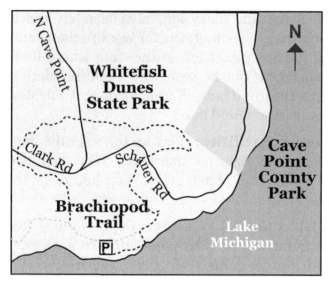

Pick up the trail from the parking lot at a fossil rock wall near the lake and follow the signs. You will cross forested dunes, considered to be the tallest on this side of Lake Michigan. The trail takes you out to a rocky shoreline with views of the lake and then bends inland through Northern Wet Mesic forests with boardwalks over wetter areas. You will eventually loop back to the parking area. This is a good choice for hiking with kids, and there is moderate interest in the signage and the sand dunes for all ages.

Trails, Access & Facilities: Pick up the 1.5-mile connector loop Brachiopod Trail from the main parking area. The park has parking, restrooms, and picnic areas. Leashed dogs are allowed.

Contact & Directions: Wisconsin Dept. Natural Resources, http://dnr.wi.gov. The park entrance is at 3275 Clark Lake Rd., Sturgeon Bay, WI 54235. Fee area.

31. Whitefish Dunes State Park – Green Trail

Whitefish Dunes State Park encompasses a great diversity of ecological communities, including some of Wisconsin's premier examples of Great Lakes Beach and Dune,

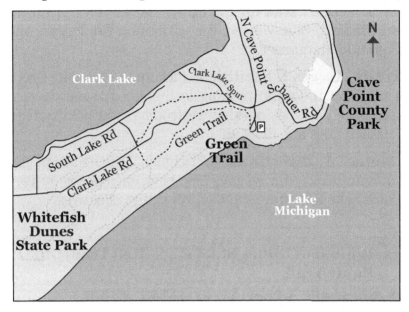

wetlands and Northern Sedge Meadow near Clark Lake, Northern Wet Mesic Forest, and Northern Mesic Forest. Many of these forests are growing atop old stabilized dunes and have a well-developed understory of native ferns and Canada Yew.

The park's 1.8-mile Green Trail traverses the back side of 'Old Baldy,' one of these ancient sand dunes. Boasting groves of towering Eastern Hemlock, White Pine, Yellow Birch, and Beech, this trail can often have abundant wildlife. Wildlife viewing in any season can be exceptional, as the park boasts a large list of mammals, including Black Bear, River Otter, Mink, and Ermine. In the summer, look for breeding Red-shouldered Hawk, Blue-headed Vireo, Chestnut-sided Warbler, Black-and-White Warbler, Ruffed Grouse, Indigo Bunting, and American Redstart. This generally easy trail is a great place to beat the summer crowds. In the off-season, you'll largely find yourself alone on these trails.

You can also take the short Clark Lake Spur, a 0.2-mile out-and-back spur to view the lake itself. Along the shores of Clark Lake, scan for the occasional families of breeding Mallard, Blue-winged Teal, Common Goldeneye, and Common Merganser.

Trails, Access & Facilities: Pick up the 1.8-mile Green Trail from the main parking lot behind the nature center. The park has parking, restrooms, and picnic areas. Leashed dogs are allowed.

Contact & Directions: Wisconsin Dept. Natural Resources, http://dnr.wi.gov. The park entrance is at 3275 Clark Lake Rd., Sturgeon Bay, WI 54235. Fee area.

32. Whitefish Dunes State Park -Red Trail/Old Baldy Trail

Ever popular Whitefish Dunes draws vacationers from all over the world during the summer months. People come to explore the park's trails and beaches. Whitefish Dunes is home to the largest sand dunes on Lake Michigan, and, depending on lake levels, its wide sandy beaches and the relatively shallow waters of Whitefish Bay make it an ideal swimming beach. Inland, the bike paths, picnic areas, and Visitor Center are also popular with vacationers.

Most popular of all is a trip along the Red Trail to Old Baldy, a 93-foot sand dune, arguably the tallest in the state.

From the top, you can see Clark Lake, Lake Michigan, and the forests beyond.

Pick up the 1.2-mile Red Trail from the main parking area at the nature center and head south through a forested dune area. The trail gradually winds its way through the well-tread beach access points higher up into the forested

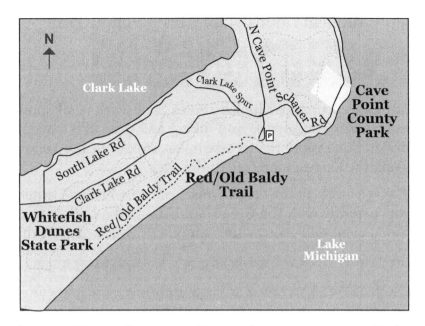

dunes. The trail gets sandier and steeper as you climb, and the park has installed some stairs with handholds and ropes to assure you in your footing up to the observation deck. On the way back down, you'll retrace your steps through the Northern Wet Mesic forests with a lush understory. While this is a well-traveled path, there is often wildlife along the trail. Keep an eye out for Ruffed Grouse, abundant in the park in some years, and listen for singing Red-eyed Vireo, American Redstart, Ovenbird, Rose-breasted Grosbeak, and Indigo Bunting, which all breed along the trail.

Trails, Access & Facilities: Pick up the 1.2 -mile Red Trail from the main parking lot behind the Nature Center.   The park has parking, restrooms, and picnic areas. Leashed dogs are allowed.

Contact & Directions: Wisconsin Dept. Natural Resources, http://dnr.wi.gov. The park entrance is at 3275 Clark Lake Rd., Sturgeon Bay, WI 54235. Fee area.

33. Whitefish Dunes State Park – Yellow Trail

For most people, Whitefish Dunes State Park is all about the beach. For anyone into hiking and especially anyone undertaking more than a few miles, check out the Yellow Trail, the longest loop trail in the park.

The 3.7-mile Yellow Trail runs from the Visitor Center, concurrently with the Green Trail, along the back side of the ancient Old Baldy dune complex. Follow it past the

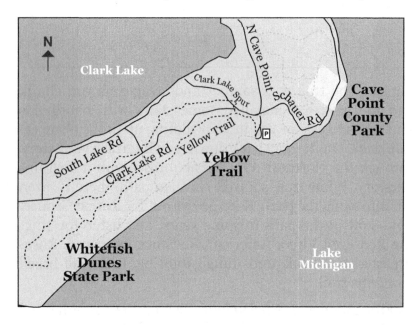

dune complex to the southwest for about 1.7 miles, before the trail bends back around to the east, crosses Clark Lake Road, and continues east for another almost 1.9 miles back to the Nature Center. You can add on the short Clark Lake Spur, a 0.2 mile out and back spur to view the lake itself. Along the shores of Clark Lake, scan for the occasional families of breeding Mallard, Blue-winged Teal, Common Goldeneye, and Common Merganser.

You will largely have the second part of the Yellow Trail to yourself, although you may occasionally hear car noise from the main park road. The trail passes through forests of Eastern Hemlock, White Pine, Yellow Birch, and American Beech and can often have abundant wildlife. Wildlife viewing in any season can be exceptional, as the park boasts a large list of mammals, including Black Bear, River Otter, Mink, and Ermine. In the summer, look for breeding Red-shouldered Hawk, Blue-headed Vireo, Chestnut-sided Warbler, Black-and-White Warbler, Ruffed Grouse, Indigo Bunting, and American Redstart. This generally easy trail is a great place to beat the summer crowds. In the off-season, you'll largely find yourself alone on these trails.

Trails, Access & Facilities: Pick up the Yellow Trail from the main parking lot behind the Nature Center. The park has parking, restrooms, and picnic areas. Leashed dogs are allowed.

Contact & Directions: Wisconsin Dept. Natural Resources, http://dnr.wi.gov. The park entrance is at 3275 Clark Lake Rd., Sturgeon Bay, WI 54235. Fee area.

EPHRAIM AND SISTER BAY

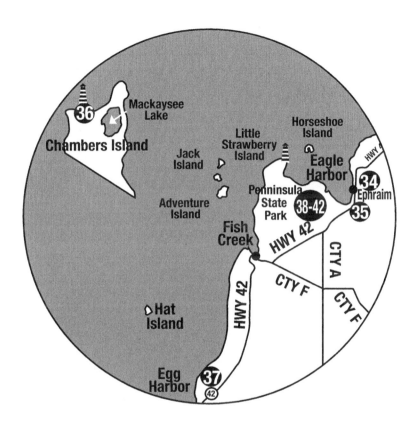

34. Ephraim Preserve at Anderson Pond

35. Ephraim Wetlands Preserve

36. Chambers Island

37. White Cliff Fen and Forest State Natural Area

38-42. Peninsula State Park

CHAPTER 6.

EPHRAIM AND SISTER BAY AREA

Ephraim, Sister Bay, Juddville, and Gibralter

The many shops, restaurants, art galleries, cultural events, festivals, and abundant natural beauty of Ephraim and Sister Bay draw hundreds of thousands of visitors each year. Eagle Harbor Lighthouse, Anderson Dock, the towering limestone cliffs of Peninsula State Park, and Old Ephraim Firehouse are must see locations for many, especially during the summer months. In July and August, when the village centers are lined with cars, and the harbors are full of boats, it is easy to see evidence of the popularity of Door County as a tourist destination.

This part of Door County has been a commercial hub for the peninsula since the mid-1800s, when the area was settled by Norwegian immigrants, who quickly set up logging operations and sawmills at Sister Bay and fished the waters of the Green Bay.

Today, the area continues to draw the crowds, including to Peninsula State Park for camping, golf, swimming, hiking, boating, and the popular outdoor Northern Lights Theater. Along with Peninsula State Park, with a multitude of marinas, and easy access to offshore islands, the area is perhaps best known as a destination for power boating, sea kayaking, sailing, and fishing, with a multitude of marinas. While this area is very popular, there is still some solitude in the great outdoors to be found if you know where to look.

34. Ephraim Preserve at Anderson Pond

Near downtown Ephraim you'll find the scenic, quiet 27-acre Door County Land Trust preserve known as Ephraim Preserve at Anderson Pond. Tucked into the woods in

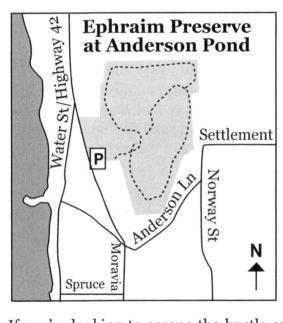

Ephraim Preserve at Anderson Pond

a residential neighborhood, this spot makes you forget that you're in the middle of Ephraim's town center.

The preserve has 1.5 miles of easy to moderate trails around the namesake Anderson Pond, an ephemeral wetland area.

If you're looking to escape the hustle and bustle of town or pass the time while friends and family dine or shop in town, this preserve is a great choice. The trails well used by local residents for dog-walking and trail running, but you'll generally have the preserve to yourself.

Pick up the 1.0-mile loop Davis Trail from the trailhead and follow it around the borders of the preserve through towering Northern Mesic woodlands. The Davis Trail's loop winds around all four corners of the parcel, making the preserve seem bigger than a mere 27 acres. When water levels are high, take the interior spur trail to Anderson Pond itself. At dawn and dusk you'll often find Little Brown Bat cruising around the pond, Raccoon, Red Fox and Virginia Opossum. In the summer, look for common breeding birds like Common Yellowthroat, Black-throated Green Warbler, Wood Duck, and American Redstart, as well for resident species like Northern Cardinal, Wild Turkey, Brown Creeper, and White-breasted Nuthatch.

Trails, Access & Facilities: This site has no facilities. There are about 1.5 miles of easy to moderate hiking trails available from the trailhead. Trails are well marked and easy to follow. Leashed dogs are permitted. Bikes, horses and motorized vehicles are prohibited.

Contact: Door County Land Trust, http://www.doorcountylandtrust.org/. 10118 Moravia St., Ephraim, WI 54211. Park off the shoulder of Moravia St. north of Anderson Ln. and follow the signs down to a kiosk and Door County Land Trust trail signage. No fee.

35. Ephraim Wetlands Preserve

This small spot, just seven acres in size, is a nice stop off to stretch your legs, and is ideally suited for a short walk with small kids or for those with limited mobility. Ephraim Wetlands Preserve is located along Hwy 42 near downtown Ephraim and managed by the Village of Ephraim for its rare native plants.

For such a small spot, the property has an interesting history. In the 1980s, the property was cleared to make way for a residential development, but after the developer walked away, local residents worked to preserve the property, and the Village put up some of the funds to preserve it as a park. Over the last few decades, trees have grown back up, and the area is transitioning to a mature Northern Wet Mesic forest, with some Northern Hardwood Swamp

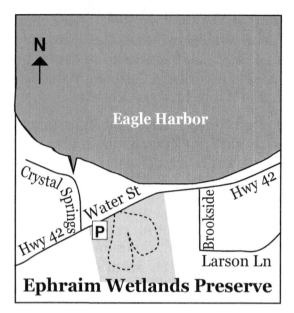

Ephraim Wetlands Preserve

pockets in wetter places. This site is primarily of interest for its spring wildflowers like Pink Lady's Slipper Orchid and Large Yellow Lady's Slipper Orchid. This spot also provides critical habitat for the endangered Hine's Emerald Dragonfly. In the spring and summer, watch for Northern Spring Peepers, Eastern Chipmunk, Grey Squirrel, American Robin, American Redstart, Chestnut-sided Warbler and Rose-breasted Grosbeak.

The preserve has two short loops, totally about 0.3 miles, with boardwalks over wetter areas. The trails are well marked and short, making it impossible to truly get lost.

Trails, Access & Facilities: There are 0.3 miles of very easy trails, boardwalks, and benches at the site with parking for about fifteen cars. There are no facilities.

Contact: Village of Ephraim, http://www.ephraim-wisconsin.com. The parking lot is located at 9820 Water St., Ephraim, WI 54204. No fee.

36. Chambers Island

If you're in the mood for a day trip offshore, or have access to a boat, Chambers Island makes a novel half day journey, and is one of our favorite day trips from the mainland. Located less than five miles offshore from Peninsula State Park, this 2834-acre island boasts a historic lighthouse and museum, which is open to the public on summer weekends.

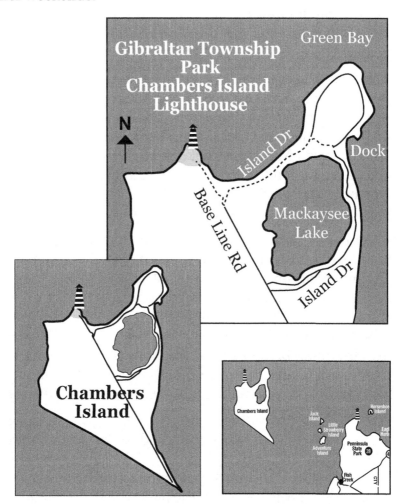

The island has a long human history, relative to this part of the world. Archeological findings on Chambers Island suggest that this island was used by Native Americans more than 10,000 years ago. Permanently settled in the mid-1800s, the island once hosted a thriving timber mill, school, and busy shipping dock.

Today, the island is a mix of private summer homes organized under the Chambers Island Association, and conservation properties owned by Door County Land Trust, with the harbor and lighthouse area managed by the Town of Gibraltar. Preservation efforts are on-going, and increasingly, local landowners are placing properties under conservation easement, and the Door County Land Trust is acquiring parcels for conservation.

This island has a mix of Northern Mesic Forest, dominated by Red Maple, Red Oak, and American Beech, and a highly productive understory, due in no small part to the removal of White-tailed Deer from the island. Inland, Chambers Island boasts Mackaysee Lake, a large freshwater inland lake, a small pond called Mud Lake, and small pockets of Northern Dry Mesic Forest pine barrens with Wild Sarsaparilla and Canada Mayflower understory.

Chambers Island supports on-going scientific activities, is an excellent place to find breeding wood warblers, including Black-throated Green, Black-and-White, Blackburnian, Chestnut-sided, and American Redstart during the summer months. Ground nesting birds like American Woodcock, Ovenbird and Black-throated Blue Warblers are also found breeding here, thanks in part to a dense understory of plants. From the shoreline, watch for Common Merganser, Osprey, Bald Eagle, American White Pelican, and Caspian Tern.

There are several miles of public roads on the island, which function as trails, and depending on lake levels, some nice sandy beaches at the north end of the island near the lighthouse. If you bring bikes on the boat, you're best suited to exploring more of the island. The classic walk is from the boat dock to the lighthouse, which takes less than an hour round-trip.

Trails, Access & Facilities: Access to the island is by private boat only. A number of local boat captains in Fish Creek offer tours out to the island, which takes about 40 minutes. Kayaking out to the island makes a challenging day trip for experienced paddlers. The lighthouse site is open to the public, managed by the Town of Gibraltar as a town park. Lighthouse tours are conducted by Door County Maritime Museum on an annual basis, and the Door County Land Trust offers tours out to the island from time to time. Roads are generally paved and flat.

Contact: Contact: Town of Gibraltar, http://www.townofgibraltar.com. Door County Maritime Museum, http://www.dcmm.org. Door County Land Trust, http://www.doorcountylandtrust.org/. No fee to visit the town park.

37. White Cliff Fen and Forest State Natural Area

White Cliff Nature Preserve, part of White Cliff Fen and Forest State Natural Area, is managed by the Door County Land Trust. This 103-acre preserve sits just north of the town of Egg Harbor along Juddville Bay and provides an easy entrée into the Door County woods from urban Egg Harbor. The fen has several short scenic loop trails, totaling about 1.5 miles, that allow visitors to walk out around the wetlands. This is a nice easy, family-friendly walk in all seasons, and the fall colors here can be gorgeous, including along the nearby rural roads.

White Cliff Fen and Forest is predominantly Northern Wet Mesic and Northern Mesic Forest bordering a Northern Sedge Meadow community. The most noteworthy fea-

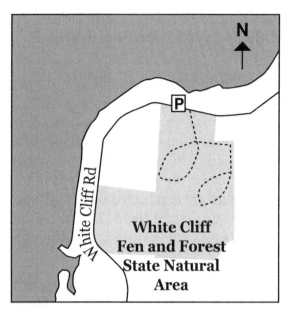

ture of the site is a spring-fed Shore Fen community located along the Niagara escarpment. Fen plants, including the rare Common Bog-Arrow Grass occur here, along with more common plants like Marsh Milkweed, Kalm's Lobelia, Swamp Goldenrod, Northern Bog Goldenrod, Marsh Marigold, and Northern Bog Aster. This is an excellent spot for Hine's Emerald Dragonfly, and butterflies like Aphrodite Fritillary and Monarch, and look for breeding birds like Rose-breasted Grosbeak, Indigo Bunting, and American Goldfinch in the summer months.

Trails, Access & Facilities: From the trailhead across from 8247 White Cliff Rd., there are approximately 1.5 miles of trails, including two loop trails. There are no facilities. Leashed dogs are permitted. Bikes, horses and motorized vehicles are prohibited. Hunting is authorized pursuant to DCLT guidelines and permission.

Contact: Door County Land Trust, http://www.doorcountylandtrust.org/. The sign and trailhead is located on the south side of the road across from 8247 White Cliff Rd., Egg Harbor, WI 54212. Additional parking is available at the nearby public boat ramp. No fee.

38. Peninsula State Park — Nicolet Bay and Hemlock Trail

Peninsula State Park was established as Wisconsin's third state park in 1909. More than a hundred years later, the park is a favorite for both visitors and Door County residents alike, drawing more than a million people annually. The park protects more than seven miles of shoreline and 3,770 acres of wetlands, meadows and forests. With a million campers, boaters, hikers, bikers, golfers, and sightseers, this park is always busy, especially in the summer months, but you can still find quiet solitude on the trails on an early morning or off-season visit.

Peninsula State Park has an excellent diversity of forest ecosystems and microclimates, and the Nicolet Bay Trail is a great way to experience that diversity. The trail passes through predominantly Northern Wet Mesic and Northern Mesic Forest communities that support a large number of forest bird species, small mammals, and amphibians. Though White-tailed Deer are present in large numbers,

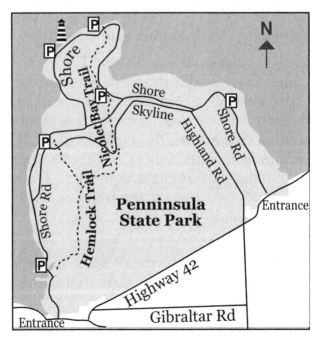

understory defoliation has not reached levels seen in some other parts of the county. As you hike through White Ash secondary growth, American Beech, Eastern White Cedar, and towering groves of massive Eastern Hemlock, look for Wild Turkey, Racoon, Northern Red Squirrel, Ovenbird, Pileated Woodpecker, and Rose-breasted Grosbeak. Weborg Marsh and Weborg Point have Emergent Marsh vegetation and sweeping views of the Green Bay, and are home to Marsh Wren, Sandhill Crane, Virginia Rail, Sora, Bald Eagle, Common Yellowthroat, Osprey, and Painted Turtle.

The Nicolet Bay Trail, which, along with a brief hop on the Hemlock Trail, totals 2.2-miles one way, or 4.4-miles roundtrip, is one of the longest, and least traveled trails in the park. These trails and moderate, and cover some rolling hills, with tree roots, mud, and loose gravel as the expected hazards. You can pick up the trail at either end, either on the north end near the parking lot at the Weckler's Point campground or at the south end at the parking lot for Weborg Point Fishing Pier, and follow the Hemlock Trail north for about 0.5 miles to pick up the official start of the Nicolet Bay Trail. Retrace your steps to return to your car.

Trails, Access & Facilities: The park has well-maintained hiking, biking, and mountain biking trails. Trail maps are available throughout the park and at the visitor center. The park also has camping, a nature center, picnic areas, a golf course, the Eagle Bluff lighthouse, boating, swimming beaches, fishing, and the Northern Sky Theater, an outdoor performing arts theater. Concessions, kayak and small boat rentals are available during the summer months. Campsites may be reserved through the Wisconsin State Parks system.

Contact & Directions: Wisconsin Dept. Natural Resources, http://www.dnr.state.wi.us. 9462 Shore Rd., Fish Creek, WI 54212. Fee area.

39. Peninsula State Park — Eagle Trail

Since its establishment in 1909, Peninsula State Park is a favorite for both visitors and residents alike. The park protects more than seven miles of shoreline, and 3,770 acres of wetlands, meadows and forests. Peninsula State Park is heavily used in the summer months by campers, boaters, hikers, bikers, golfers, and sightseers, but you can still find quiet solitude on the trails on an early morning or off-season visit.

One of the most iconic hikes in Peninsula State Park is the Eagle Trail. For more than 100 years, visitors have been taking this hike, which offers views of Eagle Harbor, and the Eagle Terrace, one of the most famous spots in all of Door County. This approximately 1.4-mile trail is one of the park's more steep and difficult trails, with rocky sections as you climb to the top of the 150-foot Eagle Bluff. Despite the effort, it is worth it. The trail passes through American Beech forests lined with Trillium, with panoramic views of the harbor below you, to the highest point in Door

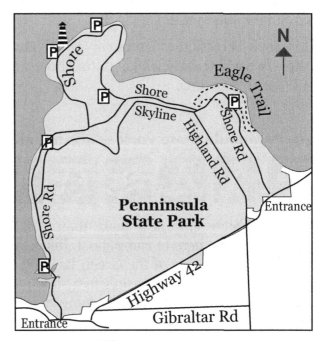

County. From the top of the bluffs, watch for migrating songbirds and raptors during the spring and fall migration, and during the summer Caspian Tern, Ring-billed Gull, Double-crested Cormorant, and Chimney Swift. These same overlooks also great places to look for migrating and wintering ducks and geese in the colder months.

You can pick up the loop trail from the parking lots at Eagle Terrace, Eagle Panorama, or Eagle Tower, and follow the loop along the lake, and then inland to return to your car. If you'd like to go a bit further, you can also add on the Minnehaha Trail to the trip.

Trails, Access & Facilities: The park has well-maintained hiking, biking, and mountain biking trails. Trail maps are available throughout the park and at the visitor center. The park also has camping, a nature center, picnic areas, a golf course, the Eagle Bluff lighthouse, boating, swimming beaches, fishing, and the Northern Sky Theater, an outdoor performing arts theater. Concessions, kayak and small boat rentals are available during the summer months. Campsites may be reserved through the Wisconsin State Parks system.

Contact & Directions: Wisconsin Dept. Natural Resources, http://www.dnr.state.wi.us. 9462 Shore Rd., Fish Creek, WI 54212. Fee area.

40. Peninsula State Park — Minnehaha Trail

Peninsula State Park sees more than a million visitors a year, who come here to camp, boat, hike, golf, and admire the clear blue waters of the Green Bay. The park was established as one of Wisconsin's first state parks more than a hundred years ago to protect more than seven miles of shoreline, and 3,770 acres of wetlands, meadows and forests.

If you are looking for an easy, family-friendly stroll in the woods within the park, the Minnehaha Trail is a good choice. This easy, 0.7-mile trail runs along Nicolet Bay between Nicolet Beach

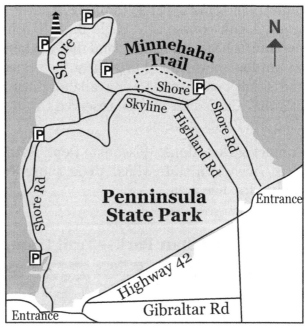

and the former site of Eagle Tower. Views of the lake, boats on the harbor, and Horseshoe Island just offshore make this a nice stroll without getting too far from the parking lot. In the summer months, out over Nicolet Bay you may see Caspian Tern, Double-crested Cormorant, Osprey, or even a Bald Eagle soaring past. In the fall look for migrating raptors like Broad-winged Hawk. In the winter, this track can be slick, but views of ice, wind, and waves of Lake Michigan crashing below make for an awesome spectacle.

You can pick up the Minnehaha Trail from the parking lots at Nicolet Beach or the South Nicolet Bay Campground. From Nicolet Beach, head southeast along the shore toward the Eagle Terrace area for about 0.7 miles. Retrace your steps to return to the car.

Trails, Access & Facilities: The park has well-maintained hiking, biking, and mountain biking trails. Trail maps are available throughout the park and at the visitor center. The park also has camping, a nature center, picnic areas, a golf course, the Eagle Bluff lighthouse, boating, swimming beaches, fishing, and the Northern Sky Theater, an outdoor performing arts theater. Concessions, kayak and small boat rentals are available during the summer months. Campsites may be reserved through the Wisconsin State Parks system.

Contact & Directions: Wisconsin Dept. Natural Resources, http://www.dnr.state.wi.us. 9462 Shore Rd., Fish Creek, WI 54212. Fee area.

41. Peninsula State Park — Trail Tramper's Delight

With its seven miles of shoreline, 3,776 acres, and iconic historic lighthouse, Peninsula State Park draws visitors from across Wisconsin and around the world. For those in search of an easy walk through the woods between the park's two most famous attractions—the Eagle Bluff Lighthouse and Nicolet Bay, try the 0.5-mile Trail Tramper's Delight.

Legend has it that this trail got its name more than a hundred years ago, in the early 1920s, then hikers named the trail for the cool shade it provided out of the hot summer sun.

You can pick up the trail at either end, near the parking lot at the Eagle Bluff Lighthouse, or the parking lot at Nicolet Bay Beach, and follow it in either direction for 0.5 miles through shady woodlands. Views on either end are great in all seasons. In summer, the spectacularly scenic blue waters of the Nicolet Bay, studded with sailboats and offering views of the surrounding Grand Traverse Islands. In the fall, this is one of the best spots on the peninsula to enjoy fall colors of orange, reds, and yellows, in contrast to the dark blue waters of the Nicolet Bay.

Along the trail listen for Red-eyed Vireo, American Redstart, and Black-and-White Warbler. While you won't have the trail to yourself, you'll be getting to the

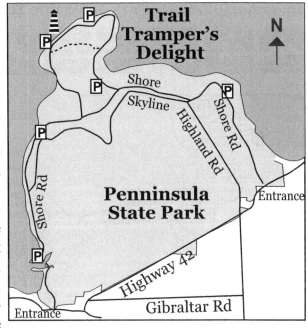

park's two most familiar attractions under your own power.

Trails, Access & Facilities: The park has well-maintained hiking, biking, and mountain biking trails. Trail maps are available throughout the park and at the visitor center. The park also has camping, a nature center, picnic areas, a golf course, the Eagle Bluff lighthouse, boating, swimming beaches, fishing, and the Northern Sky Theater, an outdoor performing arts theater. Concessions, kayak and small boat rentals are available during the summer months. Campsites may be reserved through the Wisconsin State Parks system.

Contact & Directions: Wisconsin Dept. Natural Resources, http://www.dnr.state.wi.us. 9462 Shore Rd., Fish Creek, WI 54212. Fee area.

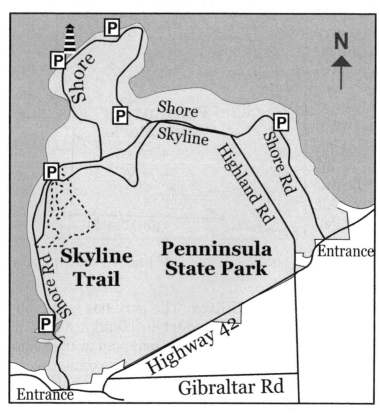

More than a million people from all corners of the world come to Peninsula State Park each year, drawn in by seven miles of shoreline, 3,776 acres, postcard perfect harbor, and historic lighthouse, but if you're looking for a bit more nature, and a few fewer people, check out the Skyline Trail.

This moderate, 3.0-mile trail, over rolling hills and up to Sven's Bluff, will take you through some of Peninsula State Park's Northern Wet Mesic and Northern Mesic Forest communities. Stone walls and the remnants of building foundations offer a glimpse into Door County's past, when this area was cleared for farming more than 150 years ago.

Along the way, look for Wild Turkey, Raccoon, Wood Frog, Red-backed Salamander, and Mourning Warbler inland, and along the lake for Caspian Tern, Osprey, and Bald Eagle cruising past on the hunt for fish.

The main draw for the Skyline Trail is the towering, rugged limestone cliffs of Sven's Bluff, the scenic vistas and birch forests the scenic vistas and birch forests of the Upper Skyline Trail. From the top of Sven's Bluff you'll look out onto the clear blue waters of the lake, and enjoy a vista made famous on a thousand Door County postcards.

You can pick up the trail from the Skyline Trail parking lot on Shore Road or the Sven's Bluff parking lot on Skyline Road. The approximately 3.0-mile loop trail is generally moderate, and traverses some hills, but it steep in places, and should only be attempted with appropriate footwear.

Trails, Access & Facilities: The park has well-maintained hiking, biking, and mountain biking trails. Trail maps are available throughout the park and at the visitor center. The park also has camping, a nature center, picnic areas, a golf course, the Eagle Bluff lighthouse, boating, swimming beaches, fishing, and the Northern Sky Theater, an outdoor performing arts theater. Concessions, kayak and small boat rentals are available during the summer months. Campsites may be reserved through the Wisconsin State Parks system.

Contact & Directions: Wisconsin Dept. Natural Resources, http://www.dnr.state.wi.us. 9462 Shore Rd., Fish Creek, WI 54212. Fee area.

BAILEYS HARBOR AREA

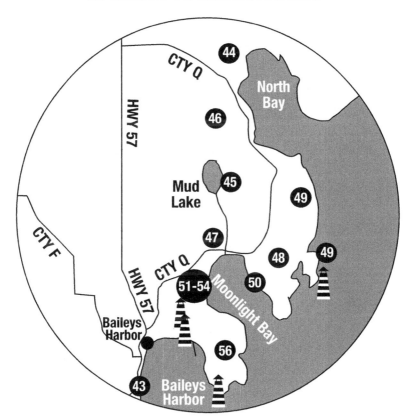

43. Bjorklunden
44. North Bay
45. Mud Lake SNA-Wetlands
46. Mud Lake SNA-Uplands
47. Mud Lake SNA-Riebolt's Creek
48. Baileys Harbor Point Boreal Forest and Wetlands SNA-Spike Horn Bay
49. Baileys Harbor Point Boreal Forest and Wetlands SNA-Cana Cove
50. Moonlight Bay Bedrock Beach State Natural Area
51 - 54. The Ridges Sanctuary
55. Logan Creek Preserve
56. Toft Point State Natural Area

CHAPTER 7.

BAILEYS HARBOR AREA

Baileys Harbor, located on the eastern "quiet side" of Door County, is a town dedicated to preservation of its natural surroundings. With thousands of acres in conservation, quiet sandy beaches, top notch fishing, three lighthouses, and a strong Great Lakes maritime tradition, Baileys Harbor is known far and wide as a place to explore Door County's outstanding scenic beauty and nature.

Once a Native American settlement, in the 1840s the area was settled by ship Captain Justice Bailey who took refuge in the harbor during a winter storm. Recognizing the potential, Captain Bailey quickly established a settlement where the group endeavored to clear the forests, quarry limestone, and convince the government to build the first of three lighthouses. By the mid- and late-1800s, the area boomed with waves of Scandinavian, English, and German settlers who built businesses, sawmills, and lime kilns, commercially fished in Lake Michigan, and set up a network of family farms in the interior. By the early 1900s, the area began to boom as a tourist destination, and many vacation homes and summer cottages were built.

One hundred fifty years later the area is still known for its summer residents, working harbor, and cherry orchards dotting the landscape. Much of the land originally cleared for timbering has returned to forest, and conservation groups have protected thousands of acres in this area for the long-term ecological benefit of the plants and animals that call this part of Door County home.

43. Bjorklunden

Owned by Lawrence University, and under a conservation easement with the Door County Land Trust, Bjorklunden is a unique place for a walk in the woods. If you're looking for something a bit outside of the norm for a weekday outing, look no further than Bjorklunden. Once a 440-acre private estate, Bjorklunden, translated from Swedish as "Birch Grove by the Lake," serves as a retreat and center for university activities and summer Shakespeare performances. It is often rented out for events like weddings and conferences, but the public is welcome to walk the trails during weekdays.

The area is a mix of mature spruce-dominated boreal forest, pockets of Eastern White Cedar, Red and Sugar Maple, and Yellow Birch forest along the shores of Lake Michigan. The trails can be exceptionally gorgeous in the fall when the leaves are turning.

Bjorklunden has about 4.0 miles of trails, including more than 0.5 miles overlooking rock terraces and small bluffs along the lake. The North Trail is generally a loop trail around the center's buildings, which you can access from either of the parking areas behind the Lodge off Boynton Lane, the main entrance road.

The Lake Trail is more scenic. You can pick up the Lake Trail on the Lake Michigan side of the Lodge. Follow the trail along the lakeshore for about 0.6 miles until it bends inland a bit for another 0.25 miles. Out and back on the Lake Trail is a bit more than a mile, but you can also take the Lake Trail to First Lane, take a left and follow that for about 0.25 miles, and then take a right to pick up the South Road for another mile back to the entrance road, and return to the Lodge, forming a loop.

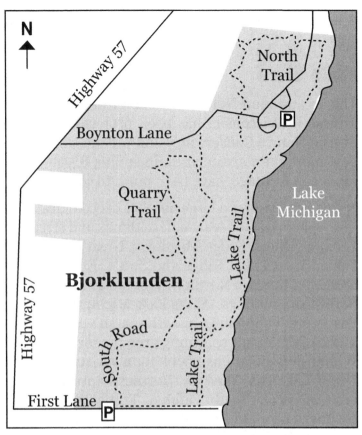

The trail itself is a typical flat broad path with some tree roots and rocks, but generally easy for all ages and abilities. Watch for White-tailed Deer, White-footed Mouse, and Eastern Bluebird in the meadows, and listen for Black-capped Chickadee, Downy Woodpecker, and White-breasted Nuthatch in the wooded areas.

Trails, Access, and Facilities: There are no public facilities. Please visit only during designated hours during weekdays and park in designated areas. Trailhead is available behind the lodge buildings.

Contact: Lawrence University. www.lawrence.edu. 7590 Boynton Lane, Baileys Harbor, WI 54202. No fee.

44. North Bay

The area around North Bay, one of the most ecologically diverse in Wisconsin, has been protected over the years by The Nature Conservancy and private landowners. Today, more than 4,700 acres, including 8,500 feet of Lake Michigan frontage, have been put into conservation.

North Bay features a large number of ecological communities: ephemeral, or seasonal, wetlands and streams, Shore Fens, Northern Sedge Meadows, Great Lakes Beach and Dune, Great Lakes Ridge and Swale, Emergent and Submergent Marshes, Northern Wet Mesic Forest, and Boreal Forest communities. Along Lake Michigan, shallow North Bay is gradually filling in with marsh vegetation, making it one of the major spawning grounds for Lake Michigan's Whitefish populations. Look for a variety of rare orchids, Dwarf Lake Iris, Muskrat, Northern Spring Peeper, Eastern American Toad, Painted Turtle, Snapping Turtle, Northern Leopard Frog, Bald Eagle, Sandhill Crane, Great Egret, Common Goldeneye, and Hine's Emerald Dragonfly.

The main part of the property has about 2.5 miles of moderate hiking trails through lush, damp Northern Wet Mesic and Boreal Forests. From the trailhead at Winding Lane, you'll proceed about 1.0 mile through dark Eastern White Cedar forests and slippery trails, across primitive boardwalks and muddy wetlands. Then, take the trail fork to the right, which will open up into a gorgeous Northern Sedge Meadow complex fringed with Tamarack trees, Dwarf Lake Iris, and a variety of other rare plants, as well as expansive views of Lake Michigan's North Bay. Depending on the season, you can walk out into the meadow toward the shoreline. In drier times of the year, you can walk to the lake's edge.

Trails, Access, & Facilities: From the parking area, the moderate 2.5-mile roundtrip trail meanders through a White Cedar swamp for about 1.0 mile before reaching a fork. If you head left, the trail will end in an adjoining private property in about 0.25 miles (not rec-

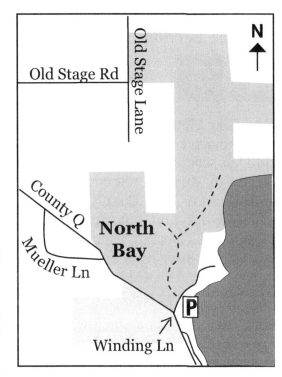

ommended). If you head right, as is recommended, the trail will go another 0.25 miles to a large Sedge Meadow along Lake Michigan. Retrace your steps to return to the parking area. The trail may be wet and has uneven sections and small wooden bridges, which may be slippery. Appropriate footwear is recommended. There are no facilities at North Bay. Bikes, dogs, and motorized vehicles are prohibited on these trails.

Contact: The Nature Conservancy, www.nature.org. The trailhead is located across from green address sign at 9804 Winding Lane, Baileys Harbor, WI 54202. Park off of the side of Winding Lane. and pick up the trailhead at the gate. No fee.

45. Mud Lake State Natural Area - Wetlands & Lake Section

Mud Lake State Natural Area, 1,200 acres, is situated between Baileys Harbor and Gills Rock. The state-owned land has several access points. The main access to the lake section of Mud Lake State Natural Area is a hidden gem in this part of Door County. It's a bit poorly marked and a bit tough to find, but rarely will you encounter another person. This location feels especially remote even though it is a quick drive from any of the towns on the Peninsula. Still the area feels wild, and one can easily imagine Black Bear roaming the wet Northern Sedge Meadows.

Mud Lake itself is a shallow, marl-bottom wetland, and water levels are variable, dependent on rainfall, and time of the year. When water levels are right, look for migrant Great Egret, Sandhill Cranes, Great Blue Herons, ducks, and geese, particularly in the fall. The lake is surrounded by

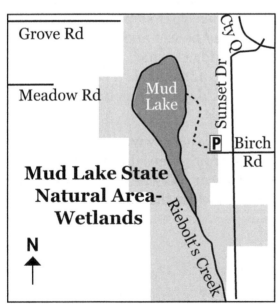

Emergent and Submergent Marsh vegetation like Bulrush, and Yellow Waterlily, and a few standing dead trees. Upland from the lake, Northern Wet Mesic Forest and Northern Hardwood Swamp communities are

interspersed with pockets of Boreal Forest.

Breeding birds include Northern Waterthrush, White-throated Sparrow, Common Goldeneye, Wood Duck, Alder Flycatcher, and Hine's Emerald Dragonfly. The shore of Mud Lake can be reached via a 1.0 mile roundtrip trail from the end of Birch Road. This trail is a double track road between two private properties and travels through old fields, a White Cedar forest, and then ends in a Northern Sedge Meadow at the lake.

Trails, Access, & Facilities: The trail is 1.0 miles round-trip to the shores of Mud Lake. There are no facilities. This area is popular with hunters in the fall.

Contact: Wisconsin Department of Natural Resources, www.dnr.state.wi.us. From the end of Birch Road, the trailhead is located across from a green address sign at 1836 Birch Road, Baileys Harbor, WI 54202. Look for the double track access road (unsigned). No fee.

46. Mud Lake State Natural Area - Upland Section

Managed by the Wisconsin Department of Natural Resources for White-tailed Deer and waterfowl hunting, the upland section of the 1,200-acre Mud Lake State Natural Area is just inland from North Bay. This section does not have access to or views of Mud Lake, but it can still provide good wildlife viewing opportunities. The 0.5-mile easy out and back hiking path from the end of Old Lime Kiln Road provides access to the meadows and wetlands, through old fields, Northern Wet Mesic Forest with pockets of Northern Hardwood and Boreal Forest, as well as wetlands areas. Listen for breeding Winter Wren, White-throated Sparrow, Alder Flycatcher, and Olive-sided Flycatcher. Mammals, including White-tailed Deer, Ermine, Northern

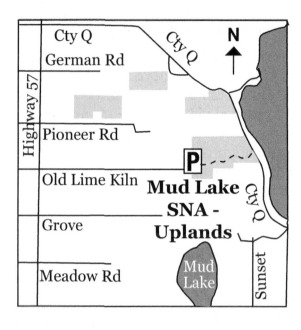

Flying Squirrel, Hoary Bat, Meadow Vole, and Mink, are all found here. Breeding warblers include Chestnut-sided, Magnolia, Yellow-rumped, Canada, Golden-winged, and Black-throated Green, along with Ovenbird, Common Yellowthroat, Northern Waterthrush, and American Redstart.

Trails, Access, & Facilities: From the end of Old Lime Kiln Road, the trailhead is located at the parking area near the WDNR sign. From the end the parking area, the trail goes about 1.0 miles roundtrip (requiring retracing of your steps to return to your vehicle). This trail provides access to the meadows but no lake views. This site has no facilities. Insect repellant is a must here during the warmer months, as mosquitoes and deer flies can be fierce at times. This site can be popular for fall deer and turkey hunting.

Contact: Wisconsin Department of Natural Resources, www.dnr.state.wi.us. The upland section of Mud Lake can be reached from by heading east on Old Lime Kiln Road until the end, at about 2050 Old Lime Kiln Road, Baileys Harbor, WI 54202, where you will see a large WDNR sign for the property. No fee.

47. Mud Lake State Natural Area - Riebolt's Creek Section

A third access point to the Mud Lake State Natural Area is off County Q. This area, managed by the Wisconsin Department of Natural Resources, includes the stretch of Riebolt's Creek flowing from Mud Lake down to the wetlands of Moonlight Bay at Lake Michigan. Along the creek you will find Red Osier Dogwoods, Willows, shrubby Northern Sedge Meadow, and extensive wetlands of Emergent Marsh vegetation. The creek is home to breeding birds and mammals including Beaver, Common Yellowthroat, Song Sparrow, Red-winged Blackbird, and Muskrat. This area is an excellent place to observe dragonflies and damselflies throughout the summer months. In the fall and winter, look for flocks of ducks and Canada Geese out on Moonlight Bay. Depending on lake levels, this area has some limited foot access but can also be visited by canoe or kayak.

By foot, depending on lake levels, there is a short, less than 0.5-mile trail, south of the County Q parking area that heads through the marsh down to Moonlight Bay and another trail on the north side of County Q

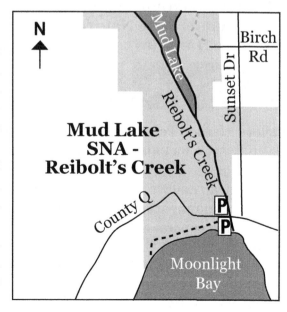

(look for the yellow State Natural Area signs) that heads north along the creek through the wetlands. When conditions are dry, you can follow the trail along the creek for quite a while, but typically much of the trail is underwater. In the spring or after rain, both trails can be wet or underwater, so appropriate footwear is essential.

Trails, Access, & Facilities: The trails are not well marked but should be obvious from the parking areas on both sides of County Q. There are no facilities.

Contact: Wisconsin Department of Natural Resources, http://www.dnr.state.wi.us/. Look for yellow State Natural Area signs indicating parking on both sides of the road where the creek crosses County Q, at about 8708 County Q, Baileys Harbor, WI 54202. There is a small parking area for about ten cars on the south (Lake Michigan) side of County Q and an additional pullout for one or two cars across the road. From Baileys Harbor, if you cross the creek and reach Sunset Drive, you've gone too far. No fee.

48. Baileys Harbor Point Boreal Forest and Wetlands State Natural Area - Spike Horn Bay

Baileys Harbor Point Boreal Forest and Wetlands State Natural Area includes a checkerboard of land managed by Wisconsin Department of Natural Resources east of Hwy Q near Baileys Harbor and along Cana Island Road between Moonlight Bay to the south and North Bay to the north. This general area has various local names, including Moonlight Bay, Cana Point, Baileys Harbor Point, Bues Point, Bues Point Landing, and probably others.

Spike Horn Bay is unique in that it has a cold microcli-

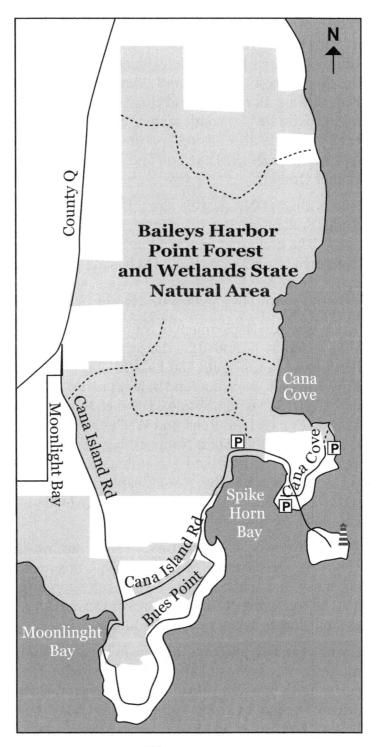

mate which allows Boreal Forest communities to coexist with Northern Wet Mesic Forest communities. In the summer, watch for breeding Blackburnian, Canada and Yellow-rumped Warblers and Common Goldeneye, along with Ermine, Porcupine, and Hoary Bat, all of which thrive here at latitudes far south of their core Canadian breeding range. This is also a good spot in spring and summer to look for rare Dwarf Lake Iris and Pink and Yellow Ladyslipper Orchids.

One of the WDNR parcels along E. Cana Island Road includes Spike Horn Bay Beach, which provides direct access to the lake and great views of the Cana Island Lighthouse in an area otherwise restricted to private property owners. Spike Horn Bay Beach features a wide, sandy beach with a characteristic Great Lakes Beach and Dune community.

The Wisconsin Department of Natural Resources owns the land generally bounded by the private homes along Bues Point Road to the south and Lake Michigan, though some private gravel operations and homes are interspersed within the WDNR's land portfolio. To reach the WDNR parcels from E. Cana Island Road and W. Cana Island Road, look for yellow WDNR State Natural Area signs. These trails are not well marked and are suited to experienced hikers ready for a healthy dose of exploration. Respect the rights of those adjacent private property owners, and do not block driveways or park on the road.

Trails, Access, & Facilities: There are no facilities. There are several miles of trails through this area, including those that reach the Lake Michigan shoreline. Trails may be confusing at times, require bushwhacking in places, and change as lake levels rise and fall.

Contact & Directions: Wisconsin Department of Natural Resources, www.dnr.state.wi.us. Park along the shoulder of E. Cana Island Road between located between the private residences at 8635 and 8739 E. Cana Island Road, Baileys Harbor, WI 54202. Access to sandy beaches can be reached by parking off E. Cana Island Road at off road parking near signage for the State Natural Area. The access to the beach is directly across the dunes via an obvious path. There are several nearby residences across from this beach. Parking on the road is prohibited, and private property rights should be respected at all times. No fee.

49. Baileys Harbor Point Boreal Forest and Wetlands State Natural Area - Cana Cove

Along Cana Island Road, between Moonlight Bay to the south and North Bay to the north, you'll find additional parcels managed by the Wisconsin Department of Natural Resources as part of the Baileys Harbor Point Boreal Forest and Wetlands State Natural Area. The parcels in this area, known locally as Cana Cove, form a checkerboard with private lands. One accessible WDNR parcel, located at the end of Cana Cove Road provides access to sweeping views of a rocky dolomite pavement ledge along the lake.

Once you're at the lakeshore, you can walk along the

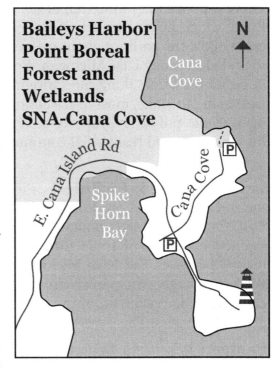

shoreline below the highwater mark to reach additional WDNR parcels to the north and west.

This area's cold microclimate, influenced by Lake Michigan, creates conditions where both Boreal Forest communities and Northern Wet Mesic Forest communities exist next to one another. Many species that normally breed in the Canadian Boreal Forests reach the southern extent of their range here. In the summer, listen for the songs of breeding birds like Canada Warbler, Blackburnian Warbler, Yellow-rumped Warbler, and Common Goldeneye, and watch for Ermine, Hoary Bat, and Porcupine.

In the spring and early summer, rare wildflowers are also present, Dwarf Lake Iris, Pink Lady's Slipper, and Large Yellow Lady's Slipper Orchids. During migration, the rocky parts of the shoreline may host migratory waterfowl like Tundra Swan and shorebirds such as Whimbrel and Greater Yellowlegs.

There is a nice 0.25-mile trail at the end of the Cana Cove Road, which heads through some scrubby Shrub Carr areas. Follow the path for about 0.1 miles to the edge of the rocky ledges along Lake Michigan. From here you can head in either direction along the shoreline. To the north and west along the lake, most of the contiguous woodlands are open to the public as property of WDNR until you reach the private, gated residential community south of Gordon Lodge Resort.

Trails, Access, & Facilities: Pick up the trailhead at the end of the Cana Cove Road cul-de-sac past the house at 8910 Cana Cove Road, Baileys Harbor, WI 54202. There are several miles of trails through this area, including those that reach the Lake Michigan shoreline. Look for WDNR signage. The parcels are not contiguous, and hikers should be respectful of the rights of adjacent private property owners. There are no facilities.

Contact: Wisconsin Department of Natural Resources,

www.dnr.state.wi.us. Access to the Cana Cove Road site can be reached by following the signs to the Cana Island Lighthouse. Trailhead is located just past the house at 8910 Cana Cove Road, Baileys Harbor, WI 54212. No fee.

50. Moonlight Bay Bedrock Beach State Natural Area

Adjacent to Baileys Harbor Point Boreal Forest lies Moonlight Bay Bedrock Beach State Natural Area, also managed by the Wisconsin Department of Natural Resources. This 5-acre rocky dolomite ledge, a great example of Great Lakes Alkaline Rockshore community, provides nice, off the beaten track access to Lake Michigan for picnicking, sunbathing, and general exploration when lake levels are low.

While there are no official hiking trails at Moonlight Bay Bedrock Beach, the exposed rock ledges are an ideal place to stretch your legs and look out at Toft Point across Moonlight Bay and take a quick walk over the rocky ledges. This is also a family-friendly alternative to Door County's typical tourist activities, so if you've kids with lots of energy after a long car trip, this spot is a great place for them to scramble around on the rocks and skip stones into

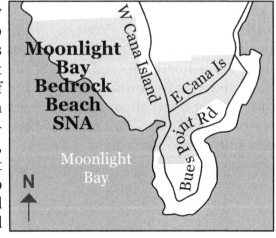

the lake.

Along the lakeshore, Boreal Forest gives way to Shrub Carr and then Northern Sedge Meadows. Inland you'll find wetlands fed by Rieboldt's Creek and Northern Wet Mesic Forest community dominated by White Cedar swamp and some smaller Tamarack swamp remnants with a few Paper Birch, White Pine, and some Northern Hardwood Swamp pockets of Black Ash. Birds like Winter Wren, Northern Parula, and Mourning Warbler can be heard on the edges of the bay during the breeding season.

Under the lake's choppy water, Moonlight Bay provides spawning habitat for Whitefish and other Great Lakes fish species. Moonlight Bay is also an important stopover site in spring and fall for Whimbrel and Tundra Swan and has pairs of breeding Bald Eagle and Osprey. In the winter months, look for diving ducks like Greater Scaup and Long-tailed Duck.

Trails, Access, & Facilities: There are no facilities. From the intersection of E and W Cana Island Road and Bues Point Road, park off the shoulder on the southeast side of the intersection, look for the sign and trailhead, and then walk west along the trail leading toward Moonlight Bay. You will reach the shoreline is less than 0.1 miles.

Contact: Wisconsin Department of Natural Resources, www.dnr.state.wi.us.   From the 3-way (stop sign) intersection of W. Cana Island Road, E. Cana Island Road, and Bues Point Road, proceed straight ahead on Bues Point Road about 50 feet until you see the brown WDNR sign on the right, at approximately 8698 Bues Point Rd., Baileys Harbor, WI 54202. Park off Bues Point Rd. on the southeast side of the intersection.   No fee.

51. The Ridges Sanctuary — Appel's Bluff

On a map of the Baileys Harbor area, the Ridges Sanctuary, also known as Baileys Harbor Ridges Sanctuary, is a swath of green. Conservation efforts in this area, leading to the creation of what is now The Ridges, began in late 1930s. In that tradition, each year naturalist staff and volunteers take thousands of visitors into the woods to learn about the area's unique geology and natural history.

The Ridges continue to evolve and add new parcels, and one of the newest additions to the preserve is Appel's Bluff along County Highway Q. Formerly part of a gravel quarry, the Appel's Bluff section of The Ridges Sanctuary was once at the bottom of an ancient lake, known as Lake Nipissing, dating to the Silurian Period, more than 400 million years ago. Quarrying in the area has left rock ledges and stone walls where fossils, including Chain Coral and Honeycomb Coral, can be found.

This 1.4-mile loop trail is accessible from its own parking lot off County Highway Q. The trail is generally a loop with an extra spur to a wetlands area and winds through ledges, Aspen and Yellow Birch groves, brushy meadows, and open fields, which can be great for butterflies in the late summer. Look

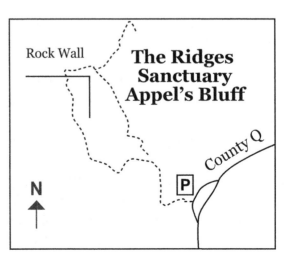

for breeding birds like Indigo Bunting, Rose-breasted Grosbeak, American Goldfinch, and Cedar Waxwing.

Trails, Access, & Facilities: The Ridges Sanctuary is also well known for its environmental education programs for both adults and children. The sanctuary is open subject to daily and seasonal hours.

Contact: The Ridges Sanctuary, www.ridgessanctuary. org. Access to this trail is from its own parking area at 8523 County Hwy Q, Baileys Harbor, WI 54202. Fee area.

52. The Ridges Sanctuary — Winter Wren Trail and Solitude Swale Loop

In addition to its status as a Wisconsin State Natural Area, the 30 glacially-formed Great Lakes Ridges and Swales at The Ridges Sanctuary are so ecologically significant they are recognized by the federal government as a National Natural Landmark.   These ridges and swales first formed about 1,200 years ago as lake levels in Lake Michigan receded. It is believed that each ridge took about 30-40 years to form. Over the last 1,200 years, Boreal and Northern Mesic Forests have grown on top of the ridges and swales, creating microclimates influenced by the cooling effect of Lake Michigan.   The result is plants and animals found here are normally found hundreds of miles to the north in the Canadian Boreal wilderness.

One of the best ways to experience these 30 ridges and swales is along the Solitude Swale Loop, which traverses a series of trails and boardwalks for 1.3 miles. Pick up the loop from the parking lot at the back entrance near the Marshall Cabin, a historic cabin on the property dating to 1854, and head east on the Winter Wren Trail, which runs

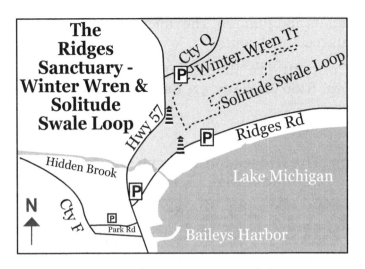

The Ridges Sanctuary - Winter Wren & Solitude Swale Loop

along Solitude Swale, one of the widest of the ridges, for about 0.6 miles. You'll then make a series of right turns, first along the Fir Trail, crossing a small boardwalk, and then onto the Labrador Trail, and then the Fir Trail again, jogging over two boardwalks. Finally, you'll make a right onto the Deerlick Trail, and follow it about 0.5 miles to the boardwalk at the Upper Range Light, where you'll make another right and follow the boardwalk north to the Marshall Cabin once again. The trails are well marked, making it hard to get truly lost, and the Upper Range Light provides a good landmark.

As you walk these trails, watch and listen for Winter Wrens, Black-throated Green Warbler, White-throated Sparrows, Northern Parulas, Red-eyed Vireos, Canada Warbler, and Black-throated Green Warblers singing from the White Spruce and Balsam Fir trees along the trails.

Trails, Access, & Facilities: The sanctuary has well-marked interpretive trails, restrooms, a Visitor Center and store, guided naturalist hikes, guided tours of the historic range lights, special events, nature programs, and volunteer opportunities. The Ridges Sanctuary is also well known for its environmental education programs for both adults and children. The sanctuary is open subject to daily and seasonal hours.

Contact: The Ridges Sanctuary, www.ridgessanctuary. org. 8166 Highway 57, Baileys Harbor, WI 54202. Fee area.

53. The Ridges Sanctuary—Hidden Brook Trail and the Range Lights

In addition to two historic lighthouses, known as the Range Lights, The Ridges Sanctuary is home to a host of animals and rare plants, a variety of more than 20 types of native orchids. The Ridges Sanctuary also boasts a long list of mammals, including Coyote, River Otter, Fisher, Grey Fox, and Black Bear. As you walk through the marshy Great Lakes Ridge and Swale communities, you'll end at the lakefront, where you may observe Caspian Terns and Double-crested Cormorants moving past along Lake Michigan. Raptors, including Merlin, Bald Eagle, and Osprey, can also be found throughout much of the year.

One of the most accessible places to see the spring and summer wildflower display and check out the Range Lights, is on the 0.6-mile (roundtrip) boardwalk trail known as the Hidden Brook Trail. This trail is accessible for all abilities and is great for kids, including kids in strollers. You can pick up the trail at the Visitor Center and follow it for 0.3 miles to the Lower Range Light. The boardwalk traverses wet areas with Showy Lady's Slipper, Yellow Lady's Slipper, and the rare Dwarf Lake Iris along both sides of the trail. These wet areas along the trails also provide critical habitat for the endangered Hine's Emerald Dragonfly. From the adjacent Black Spruce and White Spruce trees, a

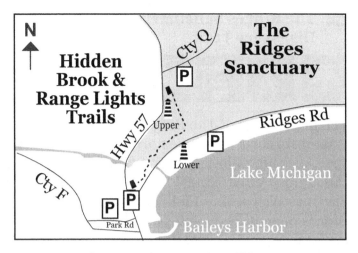

keystone species in the Boreal Forest, you'll hear the songs of 17 species of nesting wood warblers and the melodic and elusive Winter Wren.

At the Lower Range Light, you can retrace your steps back to the Visitor Center or take a left and go about 0.1 miles down the boardwalk to the Upper Range Light. These two historic lighthouses were built 1869 as a navigational aid for mariners on Lake Michigan. Today they provide summer housing for staff and have been added to the National Register of Historic Places. While you can't go inside, except on special tours, you can get up close and personal with this quirky piece of Door County's history.

Trails, Access, & Facilities: The sanctuary has well-marked interpretive trails, restrooms, a Visitor Center, store, guided naturalist hikes, guided tours of the historic range lights, special events, nature programs, and volunteer opportunities. The Ridges Sanctuary is also well known for its environmental education programs for both adults and children. The sanctuary is open subject to daily and seasonal hours.

Contact: The Ridges Sanctuary, www.ridgessanctuary. org. 8166 Highway 57, Baileys Harbor, WI 54202. Fee area.

54. The Ridges Sanctuary—Family Discovery Trail

The importance of The Ridges Sanctuary, and its place in Wisconsin conservation history, cannot be understated. In 1937, a group of local preservationists set out to preserve this unique environment, petitioning the state to recognize it as Wisconsin's first State Natural Area. Today, The Ridges Sanctuary operates as a non-profit environmental center with a small staff and a group of devoted volunteers who put in tens of thousands of hours every year to clear its trails, maintain its buildings, and spread its conservation message to visitors. In recent years, this has included both children and adult programs, turning The Ridges into a living laboratory for science, stewardship, and nature.

One of the newest parts of the program is the Family Discovery Trail, an interactive outdoor classroom, where kids can learn about plants and animals, build things, and get hands on with nature. This trail has a number of stations, each devoted to a different skill, lesson, or task. This is a fabulous activity for school-aged kids, and the trail can

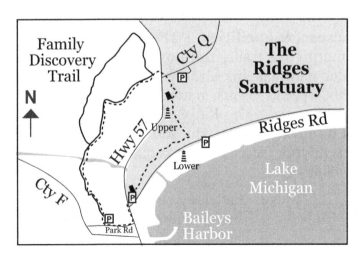

be navigated with strollers. The Family Discovery Trail is open during summer weekends. Check online for schedules and events.

Trails, Access, & Facilities: The Ridges has well-marked interpretive trails, restrooms, a Visitor Center, store, guided naturalist hikes, guided tours of the historic range lights, special events, nature programs, and volunteer opportunities. The Ridges Sanctuary is also well known for its environmental education programs for both adults and children. The sanctuary is open subject to daily and seasonal hours.

Contact: The Ridges Sanctuary, www.ridgessanctuary. org. 8166 Highway 57, Baileys Harbor, WI 54202. Fee area.

55. Logan Creek Preserve - Logan Creek State Natural Area

The Logan Creek Preserve, operated by The Ridges Sanctuary and designated as a State Natural Area, is the perfect place for a quiet walk or cross-country skiing in the winter months. The property is located along the north shore of Clark Lake and includes namesake Logan Creek, a small trout stream which feeds the lake.

Logan Creek is widely considered one of the premier places to visit in April, May, and June for orchids and other spring wildflowers. The 1.0-mile trail winds through a diversity of Northern Wet Mesic and Hardwood Swamp Forest habitats with towering stands of old growth Eastern Hemlocks, American Beech, and Red Maple. The site also features wetlands, ephemeral, or seasonal, wetlands, and a well-developed understory of plants including Canada Mayflower,

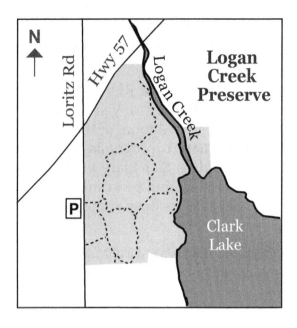

Wild Sarsaparilla, and Wood Fern. Except for spring wildflower seekers and photographers, rarely will you see others on the trails.

Spring is the best time for a visit, to see both wildflowers and migratory birds. Spring wildflowers include Trout Lily, Spring Beauty, Dutchman's Breeches, Large-flowered Trillium, and a number of native wood violets. During a morning walk during the second and third weeks of May, you can expect to see 20 or more species of migrant wood warblers, including Canada, Cape May, Blackburnian, and Bay-breasted, along with several species of vireo and all of the more common breeding resident species like Ovenbird, Rose-breasted Grosbeak, and American Redstart.

Trails, Access, and Facilities: Logan Creek has no facilities. There are 1.0 miles of trails on the property from the trailhead to the end. The trails are wide and well-maintained, and there is a kiosk at the trailhead with a trail map.

Contact: The Ridges Sanctuary, www.ridgessanctuary. org. Look for a gate marked "Tree Haven" at 5724 Loritz Road, Baileys Harbor, WI 54202. Park in the small parking lot and walk to the kiosk and trailhead. Fee area.

56. Toft Point State Natural Area

A local favorite for naturalists, artists, and hikers, Toft Point was originally settled by the Toft family in the 1870's. The family's history on the property continued for more than a 100 years, when Emma Toft, the last of the family to live at Toft Point, deeded the land for conservation purposes.

Along with The Ridges Sanctuary and Mud Lake, Toft Point is part of a larger contiguous block of undisturbed woodlands, designated as a National Natural Landmark, for the area's scenic beauty and ecological values, which are considered to be of national significance. Toft Point includes 686 acres owned by University of Wisconsin-Green Bay as a research and natural area.

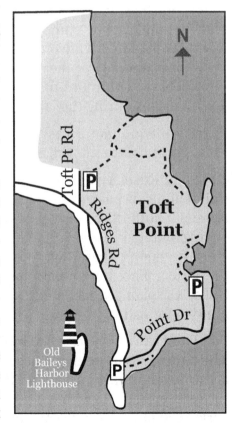

Academic research is often conducted at the site, and recent projects by professors and students from around the country range across the topics of conservation ecology, geology, hydrology, and population biology. In those studies, scientists have documented more than 440 species of plants at Toft Point.

One of the most unique features of Toft Point, and the surrounding area in general, is the pockets of Boreal Forest interspersed with Northern Wet Medsic Forest, created by the cooling effects of Lake Michigan, and ground level microclimates created by the swales and ridges that dominate the area. Toft Point, located along a peninsula jutting out into Lake Michigan, is characterized by Balsam Fir, Black Spruce, and White Spruce forests, with some White Pines, and an ecologically significant Shore Fen community with Linear-leaved Sundew and Spike Rush, rare in Door County.

These woods are home to breeding birds like Chestnut-sided Warbler, Mourning Warbler, Ovenbird, Black-and-White Warbler, Ovenbird, Magnolia Warbler, Winter Wren, Northern Parula, American Redstart, Blackburnian Warbler, and Yellow-rumped Warbler and Boreal Forest mammals like Red Squirrel, Hoary Bat, Woodland Jumping Mouse, and Porcupine. Toft Point is celebrated for its rare orchids, with more than 20 species found here, and for butterflies during the late summer and fall.

There are two main access points into the State Natural Area, Point Drive and Ridges Road.

The Point Road access point has an easy less than 1.0-mile trail that heads past grassy meadows full of summer wildflowers, butterflies, historic cabins, and a historic kiln, ending at a rocky ledge at Lake Michigan. On warm summer afternoons, these outcrops along Lake Michigan are the perfect place for sunbathing and watching Ring-billed Gulls, Caspian Terns, and Double-crested Cormorants hunting for fish.

Toft Point can also be reached by Ridges Road access point, which provides more direct access to the lakeshore, kayak launching, and views of the Old Baileys Harbor Lighthouse (private property), within easy walking distance of the parking area by parking off the road's shoulder just past the private residence at 7949 Ridges Road, which provides excellent views of the lighthouse and Lake Michigan. Note that the small peninsula out to the Old Baileys Harbor Lighthouse, and the lighthouse itself, is private property, and there is no public access.

Trails, Access, & Facilities: There are also several mostly overgrown trails to Lake Michigan and across the interior of Toft Point. For those interested in scrambling along the rocky shoreline or bushwhacking inland, there are pullouts toward the end of Point Road (no road sign). There are no facilities.

Contact: University of Wisconsin-Green Bay - Cofrin Center for Biodiversity, www.uwgb.edu. The Ridges Road trailhead is accessible from a small parking area near the residence at 7949 Ridges Road, Baileys Harbor, WI 54202. If you reach the Baileys Harbor Yacht Club, you've gone too far. To reach the Toft Point Rd. trailhead, from the end of Ridges Road, follow gravel/dirt Point Drive until the road dead ends into a parking lot and trailhead at about 7949 Point Drive, Baileys Harbor, WI 54202.   No fee.

Northern Door & Liberty Grove

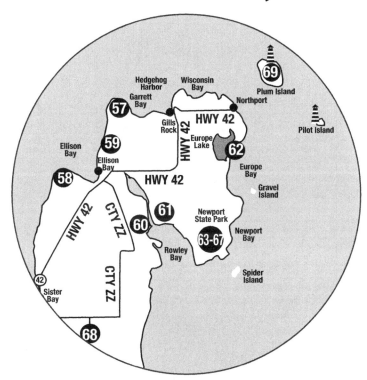

57. **Door Bluff Headlands County Park**
58. **Ellison Bluff County Park**
59. **The Clearing**
60. **Mink River Estuary - West Side**
61. **Mink River Estuary - East Side/Schoenbrunn Nature Conservancy**
62. **Newport State Park - Europe Bay Woods SNA**
63. **Newport State Park - Europe Bay Trail and Hotz Loop**
64. **Newport State Park - Newport Loop**
65. **Newport State Park - Rowleys Bay Trail**
66. **Newport State park - Lynd Point and Fern Loop**
67. **Newport State Park - Upland Connector and Upland Loop**
68. **Wilson - Three Springs Preserve**
69. **Plum Island**

CHAPTER 8

NORTHERN DOOR & LIBERTY GROVE

Northport, Rowleys Bay, Ellison Bay, Gills Rock

Ellison Bay, Northport, Rowleys Bay, and Gills Rock, at the northernmost end of the Door Peninsula, are all part of the township of Liberty Grove.

Like much of Door County, Liberty Grove was settled in the 1850s by Swedes, Norwegians, and Germans, who logged the land, quarried limestone, built shipping docks, and set up family farms in the peninsula's interior. The early days were not easy ones, with tales of logging disasters, brutally cold winters. Shipwrecks along the Portes des Mortes (Death's Door) separating Gills Rock from Washington Island dominate the early history of the area. These isolated communities hung on due to their location along the Great Lakes shipping routes and the abundant natural resources such as timber, beaver and muskrat, and limestone.

Today, Liberty Grove continues its agricultural and maritime tradition. Driving the country roads, you'll pass small family farms growing wheat, cherry and apple orchards, and many second homes and summer cottages. Along the lake, the settlements of Northport and Gills Rock are known for their working harbors, charter fishing opportunities, and ferries to Washington Island. Offshore islands provide habitat for breeding birds, and the natural diversity of the Northern Door is evident even to casual observers.

With its deserted beaches, scenic harbors, picturesque lighthouses, and 45 miles of shoreline, Liberty Grove has a bit of a sleepy reputation. The primary draw is Newport State Park for hiking, camping, and mountain biking. In addition to the 30 miles of trails at Newport State Park, there are a host of other spots to visit in Liberty Grove, whether you stay for the day, the week, or much longer.

57. Door Bluff Headlands County Park

Door Bluff Headlands, 155 acres, operated as a Door County Parks System park, is located at the northwestern-most point of the Door Peninsula near Ellison Bay. The park has a notable place in history as a site of conflicts between rival Iroquois and Potawatomi tribes. Door Bluff Headlands County Park is also famous for its Potawatomi tribal pictographs etched into the limestone cliffs along Lake Michigan and are still visible today if you access the site by boat. The park is also noteworthy for its spectacular limestone bluffs towering over Green Bay, which give you impressive vistas of Lake Michigan and the offshore islands.

As you walk the damp, dark trails of towering Eastern White Cedar, it's easy to imagine how things may have looked to those early Native American tribes. The forest blocks out the sunlight, even on the longest summer days, making Door Bluff Headlands County Park seem particularly remote. Atop the bluffs, you'll stand at one of the highest elevations in Door County. Offshore, glimpse views of Washington Island and the Plum Island lighthouse through the massive, ancient forests growing precariously from the fragile soil atop the bluffs as you gaze out on Hedgehog Harbor.

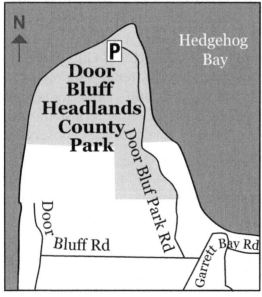

This park is perfect for those in search of outdoor adventure. While trails are not well marked or maintained by the county, there is an extensive network of trails on the property, and intrepid hikers can find several miles of steep and often rocky trails down to views of the lake. Given the small size of the park, it's difficult to truly get lost, but remember to be cautious, as there are many dangerous outcrops and slippery slopes without guard rails that could send you tumbling off a cliff.

In the summer, the park is home to breeding birds like Rose-breasted Grosbeak, Great Crested Flycatcher, Hermit Thrush, Indigo Bunting, and Red-eyed Vireo. Lucky visitors may also spot mammals like Big Brown Bats, Porcupine, Virginia Opossum, or Raccoon, especially just before sunset. During spring migration, look for migrant songbirds in the trees and along the park roads.

Trails, Access, & Facilities: The park has a seasonal restroom, parking along the road, and a network of unofficial hiking trails throughout the property. There are currently no marked trails. The park provides lake views through the trees, but it is primarily wooded.

Contact: Door County Parks System, http://map.co.door.wi.us/parks/. 12900 Door Bluff Park Road, Gills Rock, WI 54210. No fee.

58. Ellison Bluff County Park

Ellison Bluff County Park is one of our absolute favorite parks in the Door County Parks System, featuring towering bluffs along the Niagara Escarpment. The park is also a Wisconsin State Natural Area noted for its ecological diversity. This scenic 174-acre park is best known for the over-

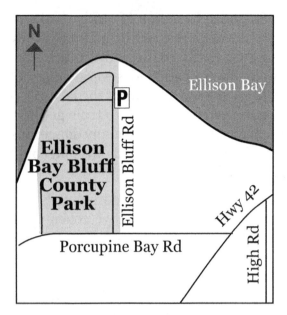

look platform atop its 180-foot tall Ellison Bluff, which provides panoramic Green Bay views of Chambers Island, Chambers Island, Horseshoe Island, the Strawberry Islands, and on clear days, the Upper Peninsula of Michigan.

The viewing overlook atop the main bluff tends to draw crowds, but for those visitors interested in a bit more, you can walk the series of short gravel walking trails.

Along the trails you'll find plants on the forest floor including Canada Mayflower, Wood-Betony, Bracken Fern, Large-flowered Trillium, and Wild Sarsaparilla, and more than 25 species of native snails. Listen for birds such as Rose-breasted Grosbeak, Scarlet Tanager, Great-crested Flycatcher, and Winter Wren, and keep an eye out for Grey Fox, Raccoon, Northern Flying Squirrel, and Ermine.

Trails, Access, & Facilities: The park has a network of easy, short easy hiking trails off a central 1.0-mile loop trail. The trails are gravel and well marked. The park has lots of parking, picnic areas, restrooms, and an overlook platform.

Contact: Door County Parks System, http://map.co.door. wi.us/parks/. 12050 Ellison Bluff Road, Ellison Bay, WI 54210. No fee.

59. The Clearing

The Clearing is one of our absolute favorite places in Door County to take a class or a walk in the woods. Formerly the estate of Jens Jensen, The Clearing offers folk arts classes throughout the year but also opens up on weekend afternoons in the summer for docent-led hikes.

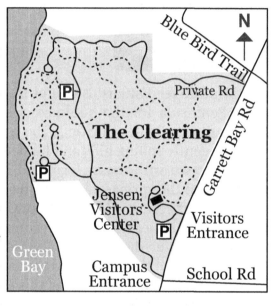

As you wander the property marveling at the towering Red Cedars growing out of the rock outcrops of the Niagara Escarpment, the well-designed landscaping features, and the scenic vistas, you'll find a quiet sense of self-reflection and connection with nature. Along the way, watch for Porcupine, American Woodcock, and Pileated Woodpecker. Listen for Ovenbird and American Redstart singing on territories from the forests, Eastern Bluebirds, Song Sparrows, and Tree Swallows nesting in the meadows, and maybe even a Striped Skunk, Racoon, or Porcupine.

The Clearing has about a mile of trails across its 125 acres. These are generally flat, easy, and include mowed paths through the main Inner Meadow and Hay Meadow, which change a bit from year to year, and forest trails along Lake Michigan. Paths also head down behind the Lodge to the shores of Lake Michigan.

Trails, Access, & Facilities: Park at the Visitor Center, open on weekend afternoons. Please be respectful of private property, and only visit during designated hours.

Contact: The Clearing www.theclearing.org. 12171 Garrett Bay Road, Ellison Bay, WI 54210. No fee to walk the trails.

60. Mink River Estuary – West Side

The Mink River Estuary is one of the best places on the Door Peninsula for the outdoors, whether it be hiking, kayaking, or wildlife-watching. The trails are quiet, passing over gently rolling hills and hidden wetlands, through forests strewn with mossy logs, and finally ending along the banks of the spring-fed Mink River. This is one of the top places for seeing wildlife in Door County at all times of the year, and it's a great spot to reconnect with the natural world, no matter the season. The west side of the Mink River was one of the first places protected in Door County by The Nature Conservancy, and this group has added significant acreage to its holdings over time. The west side is a bit less traveled than the east side and is highly recommended for any Door County hiker.

The Mink River is really more of a bay of Lake Michigan, emptying into the lake at Rowleys Bay, than it is a true river. It is one of the few substantial estuaries of Lake Michigan in this part of the state, making it an important area for spawning fish and other wildlife. Along the Mink River you'll find a large Emergent Marsh community, dominated by Bulrush, Wild Rice, and Cattail.

Water levels in the Mink River and the estuary's marshes fluctuate depending on seasons and weather conditions and are often flooded by seiches, or sloshing waves, from Lake Michigan. Inland and along the Mink River, vegetation is Northern Sedge Meadow community, bordered by Willow and Alder thickets, which grad-

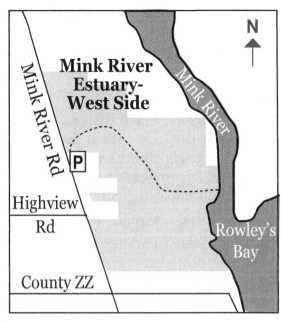

ually gives way to a Northern Wet Mesic Forest. Breeding plants and animals include Hine's Emerald Dragonfly, Beaver, Muskrat, Northern Flying Squirrel, Meadow Jumping Mouse, Northern Spring Peeper, and occasionally a River Otter, along with nesting Wood Duck, Blue-winged Teal, Great Blue Heron, and Wood Thrush. Tundra Swans, Sandhill Cranes, and migrant waterfowl may be found in and around the wetlands during the migration periods.

There are about 5.0 miles of trails on the west side of the river. The uncrowded, scenic, Maple Ridge Trail winds through the property, branching off into several other trails, including the Rowley's Bay Trail, the Mink River Trail, and the Little Pond Trail. The trails on the preserve are wide, two-track, with the exception of the overgrown, narrow Little Pond Trail.

We recommend the approximately 2.3-mile roundtrip Maple Ridge to Mink River Trail, an easy to moderate walk from the parking area to the river. The trail passes through an impressive mix of towering old Eastern White Cedar forests and mixed deciduous Northern Mesic communities, ending with spectacular views of the Emergent Marshes. From the parking on Mink River Road follow the Maple Ridge Trail to the Mink River Trail. Follow the Mink River Trail until you reach the river. Retrace your steps to return to the parking area.

Trails, Access, & Facilities: There are about 5.0 miles of trails on the west side of the river. There are no signs at the trailheads, but there are a few signs throughout the property. The preserve has no facilities. Bikes, dogs, and motorized vehicles are prohibited on these trails.

Contact: The Nature Conservancy, www.nature.org. There is a small parking lot for the Nature Conservancy preserve, located across the street between the green address signs for 11713 and 11723 Mink River Road, Ellison Bay, WI 54210, near the junction with Sylvan Lane. No fee.

61. Mink River Estuary – East Side/Schoenbrunn Nature Conservancy & Rowleys Bay

The east side of the Mink River, also known as the Schoenbrunn Conservancy, is ideal for a quiet hike and is not to be missed if you're into wildlife viewing. The Nature Conservancy also owns substantial holdings on this side of the river down to the mouth of the river at Rowleys Bay. Beginning at Rowleys Bay, the east side of the Mink River Estuary is also an ideal launching point for a sublime paddling experience.

The spring-fed Mink River is really more of a bay of Lake Michigan than it is a true river. This area contains a mix of ecological communities, making it an excellent place to view wildlife. The areas along the Mink River contain a large Emergent Marsh community, dominated by Bulrush, Wild Rice, and Cattail, which are critical spawning areas for some of Lake Michigan's popular sport fishing species.

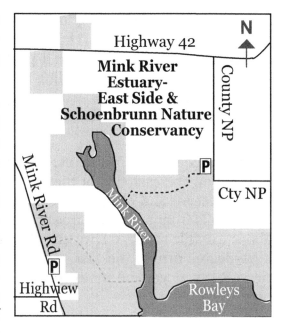

The Lake Michigan shoreline and beach at Rowleys Bay contain a significant Great Lakes Ridge and Swale community that includes abundant spring wildflowers, several types of rare orchid, and Dwarf Lake Iris. Water levels in the Mink River and the estuary's marshes fluctuate depending on seasons and weather conditions. While there are no true tides in Lake Michigan, the Mink River is often flooded by back and forth sloshing waves known as seiches, from Lake Michigan which function in a similar manner.

Inland and along the Mink River, you'll find a Northern Sedge Meadow community, bordered by Willow and Alder thickets, which gradually gives way to a Northern Wet Mesic Forest community. Look for Hine's Emerald Dragonfly, Beaver, Muskrat, Northern Flying Squirrel, Meadow Jumping Mouse, Northern Spring Peeper, and occasionally a River Otter, along with nesting Wood Duck and Blue-winged Teal, Great Blue Heron, Wood Thrush, and Sandhill Cranes. During spring and fall migration, Tundra Swans, ducks, and geese may be found in large flocks along the mouth of the river at Rowleys Bay.

The main west side trail is known as the Hemlock Trail,

which begins at the parking lot and heads directly to the banks of the Mink River. The trail is an easy 1.75-mile roundtrip. Along the way, you'll pass through towering Northern Mesic forests, including several stands of large old-growth Hemlock trees. The trail ends in an open area along the river and provides excellent views of the marshes.

Trails, Access, & Facilities: There are several miles of trails on the east side of the river on TNC's Schoenbrunn Preserve and along Rowleys Bay. You can access these trails from a parking area at the bend of County NP about 1.0 mile south of Hwy 42, where County NP makes a 90-degree turn to the east. The preserve has no facilities. Bikes, dogs, and motorized vehicles are prohibited on these trails.

Contact: The Nature Conservancy, www.nature.org. The parking area is at the 90-degree turn in County NP at about 999 County Highway NP, Ellison Bay, WI 54210. No fee.

62. Newport State Park – Europe Bay Woods State Natural Area

Europe Bay Woods State Natural Area is 200 acres and is situated along an isthmus between Lake Michigan and Europe Lake at the very northern edge of Newport State Park. The area is noted for both its exceptional diversity of wildlife, earning it a state natural area designation, and its scenic beauty. The area is accessible from the Newport State Park trail system via Europe Bay/Hotz Lake Loop Trail and features the quiet Europe Lake shoreline on one side and Lake Michigan beaches on the other.

If you make it to Europe Bay Woods State Natural Area,

chances are good that you'll generally have the place to yourself for a quiet walk along a scenic Lake Michigan beach. The undeveloped beach has low dunes and large eroded stone ledges when water levels are low. It is ideal for

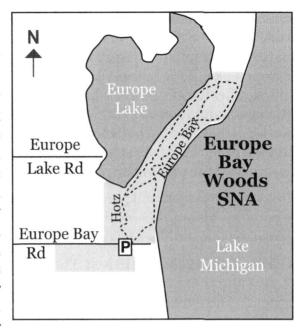

swimming, albeit a little chilly even in the late summer! This is one of the quietest beaches in all of Door County and is perfect for anyone looking to get away from the crowds.

Europe Bay Woods contains a mix of ecological communities, including spruce-dominated Boreal Forest, mixed deciduous Northern Mesic Forest, and pine-dominated Northern Dry Mesic Forest. Plants found along the forest floor include Beaked Hazelnut, Wintergreen, Wild Sarsaparilla, Dwarf Lake Iris, and Canada Mayflower. Europe Bay Woods is home to birds and animals, including Black-throated Blue and Cape May Warblers, Striped Skunk, Red Bat, Ermine, Hoary Bat, Porcupine, Grey Fox, Snowshoe Hare, Wild Turkey, Ruffed Grouse, and Red Fox.

The closest parking area is at a small Liberty Grove town park, located at the end of Europe Bay Road with access to the beach. From the parking area at the beach, you can backtrack along Europe Bay Road for a few hundred feet until you reach the Europe Bay Trail (part of Newport State

Park's trail system), which runs along Lake Michigan, or backtrack even further inland along Europe Bay Road for about 0.2 miles to Hotz Loop Trail, which runs along Europe Lake. Both Europe Bay Trail and Hotz Loop Trail run parallel to one another, both north-south along Lake Michigan, and intersect with one another at the northern border of Newport State Park. You can take one trail north and the other south or retrace your steps on the same trail to return to the parking area.

For a much longer walk, you can also access Europe Bay Woods by hiking the entire Europe Bay Trail and Hotz Loop (see hike number 63 below).

Trails, Access, & Facilities: Trails through Europe Bay State Natural Area are part of the Newport State Park trail system. The entire Europe Bay Trail and Hotz Loop provide about 7.0 miles of hiking and biking trails and include the trails through the State Natural Area portions of Newport State Park. There are no facilities within the Europe Bay State Natural Area boundaries; however, Newport State Park provides picnic areas, restrooms, drinking water, and shelters. Campsites may be reserved through the State of Wisconsin Parks system.

Contact: Wisconsin Department of Natural Resources, http://www.dnr.state.wi.us/. The nearest parking to Europe Bay Woods State Natural Area is at Liberty Grove Town Park, 350 Europe Bay Road, Ellison Bay, WI 54210. The main Newport State Park entrance is at 475 County Highway NP, Ellison Bay, WI, 54210. Fee area.

63. Newport State Park – Europe Bay Trail and Hotz Loop

In comparison to the other state parks on the peninsula, Newport is relatively crowd-free. The hiking trails are also plentiful, and aside from a few campers, you will generally have the place to yourself. The moderate Europe Bay Trail and Holtz Loop, 7.0 miles in total, are widely considered the most iconic hike in Newport State Park. It is also the longest we've found in any of the Door County State Parks.

The Europe Bay and Hotz Loop Trail runs through the Europe Bay Woods State Natural

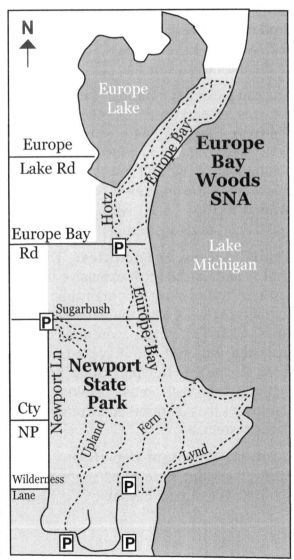

Area, one of the most scenic spots in the park (which we detail at hike number 62 in this book). Along the trail, you'll walk across forested woodlands situated atop ancient ridges, swales, and low wooded ridges interspersed with wetlands. Along Europe Lake, look for Common Merganser, Red-breasted Merganser, Wood Duck, and Common Goldeneye. Along Lake Michigan, watch for Caspian Tern, Double-crested Cormorant, Ring-billed Gull, and Herring Gulls. These birds can all be observed nesting offshore at Spider and Gravel Islands. You might also spy Bald Eagle and Osprey. In some years, the Ruffed Grouse population in the park is substantial.

You can pick up the trailhead at Parking Lot 5 near the picnic area, or park in Parking Lot 3 at Europe Bay Road (in the spaces designated for campsite access). This trail will take you past the three most coveted campsites in the park – numbers 14, 15, and 16. These sites are tucked in along the shore of Europe Lake. Note that the trail, particularly around Europe Lake, can be buggy in the summer, and you'll want to douse yourself in strong bug spray.

Trails, Access, & Facilities: The Newport State Park trail system is the most extensive in Door County. Some of these trails allow mountain biking; others are limited to hiking. Check with the park Visitor Center for specific rules. Lake Michigan swimming beaches are accessible from the trail system. Kayaks can be launched directly from the beach. Newport State Park provides camping, picnic areas, restrooms, drinking water, and shelters. Campsites may be reserved through the State of Wisconsin Parks system.

Contact: Wisconsin Department of Natural Resources, http://www.dnr.state.wi.us/. 475 County Road NP, Ellison Bay, WI 54210. Fee area.

64. Newport State Park—Newport Loop

Newport State Park offers one of the best chances for one of the more remote nature experiences in all of Door County. Even during the high season, the trails and wide, wind-swept Lake Michigan beaches at Newport State Park are generally empty. On most days you'll practically have the place to yourself.

For those in search of a good workout, moderately challenging terrain, and a nice walk through the woods, we especially recommend the moderate Newport Loop, which totals about 5.0 miles. The Newport Loop passes through the Newport Conifer Hardwoods State Natural Area, a Northern Mesic Forest situated atop a long, rocky dolomite ledge, complete with boulders, ancient dunes, and

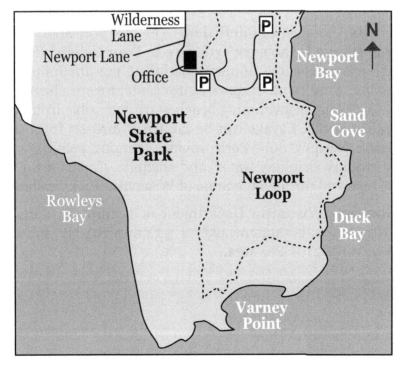

some pockets of Boreal Forest. This 5-mile loop trail begins at the picnic area and travels to the southern part of the park with access to campsites and has some obscured views of Lake Michigan through the forests of American Beech, Sugar Maple, Eastern Hemlock, Balsam Fir, Eastern White Cedar, and White Spruce.

Along the trail, you'll traverse three to eight-foot dolomite ledges with embedded fossils that date to the former shoreline of the ancient Lake Nippissing stage of Lake Michigan. Listen for the sounds of breeding Great-crested Flycatcher, Red-eyed Vireo, Winter Wren, American Robin, Cedar Waxwing, and Scarlet Tanager.

Pick up the trail from Parking Lot 2, and head south along the southern edge of the park along Lake Michigan. The well-marked Newport Loop runs past key parking landmarks along Lake Michigan like Sand Cove, Duck Bay, and Varney Point before returning north up the middle and back to Parking Lot 2.

Trails, Access, & Facilities: The Newport State Park trail system is the most extensive in Door County. Some of these trails allow mountain biking; others are limited to hiking. Check with the park visitor center for specific rules. Lake Michigan swimming beaches are accessible from the trail system. Kayaks can be launched directly from the beach. Newport State Park provides camping, picnic areas, restrooms, drinking water, and shelters. Campsites may be reserved through the State of Wisconsin Parks system.

Contact: Wisconsin Department of Natural Resources, http://www.dnr.state.wi.us/. 475 County Rd. NP, Ellison Bay, WI 54210. Fee area.

65. Newport State Park—Rowleys Bay Trail

Newport State Park is the first place in Wisconsin to be designated an International Dark Sky Park, testament to the park's remoteness. One of Newport State Park's best off-the-beaten track hikes is the Rowleys Bay Trail, a moderate 4.0-mile trail along the southwestern boundaries of the park, along the namesake Rowleys Bay.

On most days you'll have the Rowleys Bay Trail to yourself. This area has extensive Northern Mesic Forest and some pockets of Boreal and Northern Wet Mesic Forests. In the forests, watch for Porcupine, Mink, Grey Fox, Hoary Bat, Northern Flying Squirrel, Red Squirrel, Snowshoe Hare, White-throated Sparrow, Warbling Vireo, Winter Wren, Red-shouldered Hawk, Cooper's Hawk, Merlin, Magnolia,

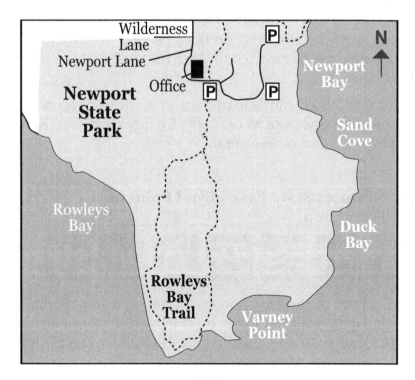

Chestnut-sided Yellow-rumped, and Black-throated Green Warblers, Ovenbird, Hermit Thrush, and American Redstart. Canada Warbler is also present in low numbers, and along Rowleys Bay keep an eye out for ducks and geese, particularly during spring and fall migration.

You can pick up the Rowleys Bay Trail from Parking Lot 1, and head south through the interior forests for about 1.9 miles before reaching campsite number 10. As the path forks, head to the right, where you'll see additional campsites 11, 12, and 13, all situated at the edge of Rowleys Bay. The trail then winds its way north back through the park's interior for about another 2.0 miles.

Trails, Access, & Facilities: The Newport State Park trail system is the most extensive in Door County. Some of these trails allow mountain biking; others are limited to hiking. Check with the park Visitor Center for specific rules. Lake Michigan swimming beaches are accessible from the trail system. Kayaks can be launched directly from the beach. Newport State Park provides camping, picnic areas, restrooms, drinking water, and shelters. Campsites may be reserved through the State of Wisconsin Parks system.

Contact: Wisconsin Department of Natural Resources, http://www.dnr.state.wi.us/. 475 County Road NP, Ellison Bay, WI 54210. Fee area.

66. Newport State Park—Lynd Point to Fern Loop

Particularly in the busy summer months, it can be challenging to find shorter hikes, especially with lake views, at Door County's state parks that aren't totally overrun with people. One of your best opportunities for a shorter loop with plenty of scenery and few crowds, is the Lynd Point to Fern Loop portion of Newport State Park.

Lynd Point to Fern Loop, on Newport's Lake

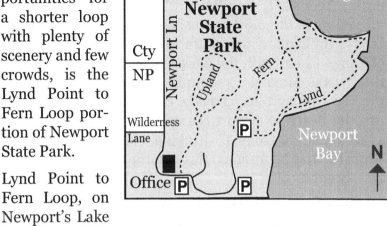

Michigan shoreline, offers one of the best chances for a more remote nature experience. Even during the high season, the trails are wide and wind-swept Lake Michigan beaches at Newport State Park are generally empty. On most days you'll practically have the place to yourself.

The area around Lynd Point and Fern Loop is also one of the coolest places on the entire Door Peninsula, temperature-wise. This area boasts Northern Mesic Forest and some pockets of Boreal and Northern Wet Mesic Forests. In the forests, watch for birds like Warbling Vireo, Winter Wren, Ovenbird, Red-shouldered Hawk, White-throated Sparrow, Cooper's Hawk, Merlin, Magnolia, Chestnut-sided Yellow-rumped, and Black-throated Green Warblers, Hermit Thrush, and American Redstart and animals including Porcupine, Hoary Bat, Northern Flying Squirrel, Mink, Grey Fox, Red Squirrel, and Snowshoe Hare.

Pick up the 2.2-mile trail at Parking Lot 3 near the picnic area. You'll first loop out due east along the namesake Lynd Point, which juts into Lake Michigan for about 1.0 miles. Eventually you'll come to Campsites 1 and 2, at the tip of Lynd Point, before turning back south through the interior reaches of the park back to the picnic area, just over 1.1 miles.

Trails, Access, & Facilities: The Newport State Park trail system is the most extensive in Door County. Some of these trails allow mountain biking; others are limited to hiking. Check with the park Visitor Center for specific rules. Lake Michigan swimming beaches are accessible from the trail system. Kayaks can be launched directly from the beach. Newport State Park provides camping, picnic areas, restrooms, drinking water, and shelters. Campsites may be reserved through the State of Wisconsin Parks system.

Contact: Wisconsin Department of Natural Resources, http://www.dnr.state.wi.us/. 475 County Road NP, Ellison Bay, WI 54210. Fee area.

67. Newport State Park – Upland Connector and Upland Loop

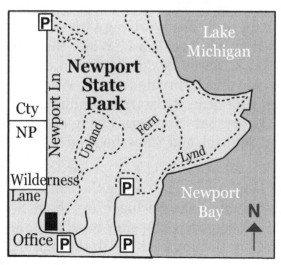

In comparison to the other state parks on the peninsula, Newport is relatively crowd-free. The hiking trails are also plentiful, and aside from a few campers, you will generally have the place to yourself.

The easy Upland Loop, a 1.5-mile loop trail, is suitable for hiking with kids or those who can't walk as far but still want to get a good workout. This trail looks more like the other state parks in Door County and less like the Boreal Forest found in other parts of Newport State Park. This is a great place to find Ruffed Grouse, Chestnut-sided Warbler, Red-eyed Vireo, and the occasional Mourning Warbler.

The Upland Connector begins near the park office off the main road and synchs up with the Upland Loop in about 0.25 miles. The trail is well-marked and easy to follow. The Upland Loop is generally flat and easy, passing through old fields on a two track at first, and then narrowing, it will take you through open Northern Mesic forests with lots of secondary growth.

Trails, Access, & Facilities: The Newport State Park trail system is the most extensive in Door County. Some of these trails allow mountain biking; others are limited to hiking. Check with the park Visitor Center for specific rules. Lake Michigan swimming beaches are accessible from the trail system. Kayaks can be launched directly from the beach. Newport State Park provides camping, picnic areas, restrooms, drinking water, and shelters. Campsites may be reserved through the State of Wisconsin Parks system.

Contact: Wisconsin Department of Natural Resources, http://www.dnr.state.wi.us/. 475 County Road NP, Ellison Bay, WI 54210. Fee area.

68. Wilson-Three Springs Preserve

Harold C. Wilson Three Springs Preserve, managed by the Door County Land Trust, is a 515-acre parcel that protects

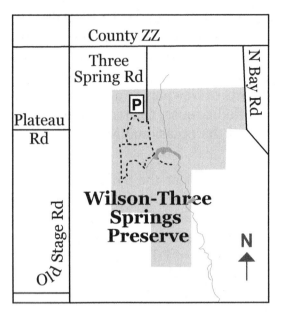

the headwaters of the Three Springs Creek. The preserve sits within the North Bay wetlands complex, which feeds into North Bay. Wilson-Three Springs Preserve contains a diversity of habitat types, including Northern Sedge Meadows, Emergent Marshes, Northern Wet Mesic Forest, seasonal streams, and Submergent Marshes.

The area harbors a variety of wetlands-associated plants and animals including a variety of dragonflies such as the endangered Hine's Emerald Dragonfly. Also found in this area are species such as Bald Eagle, American Bittern, Belted Kingfisher, Muskrat, Meadow Vole, Sandhill Crane, Great Blue Heron, White-tailed Deer, rare orchids, and Dwarf Lake Iris. Three Springs Creek, North Bay, and the adjacent wetlands also provide critically important habitat for some of Door County's most significant sport fishing populations including Chinook Salmon, Smallmouth Bass, Brown Trout, Northern Pike, Yellow Perch, and Lake Michigan Whitefish.

The meadows and wetlands at Wilson-Three Springs Preserve can be particularly noteworthy in the late summer and early fall for wildflowers and butterflies. The property has an easy looping circuit of about 1.75-mile roundtrip loop trails and interpretive kiosk at the trailhead. The trail heads from the parking area, past scenic meadows and historic buildings, and ends at marshes around the springs after about 0.5 miles, with two additional loops of about an additional 1.25 miles if you want to walk a bit further, for a roundtrip total of about 1.75 miles. For a quick out and back trip to the springs, you can also retrace your steps to return to your car, for a total hike of about 1.0 mile.

Trails, Access, & Facilities: This preserve has no facilities. Hunting is authorized pursuant to DCLT guidelines and permission.

Contact: Door County Land Trust, http://www.doorcountylandtrust.org/. Head south on Three Springs Rd., a gravel track with a few houses along it. At the end of Three Springs Road, about 10422 Three Springs Road, Sister Bay, WI, 54234, you will see a Door County Land Trust sign and trailhead. No fee.

69. Plum Island – Landing to Range Lights

Plum Island, one of the Grand Traverse Islands, is a 325 acre uninhabited former Coast Guard owned property best known for its historic lighthouse and boathouse, visible to anyone taking the ferry out to Washington Island.

Until recently, the island was off limits to the public. In recent years, the island's upkeep has transferred over to the Green Bay National Wildlife Refuge, and a group of volunteers is working to restore the historic buildings, lighthouse, and other infrastructure.

This is an excellent place to observe nature, including birds like Double-crested Cormorant, Caspian Tern, Bald Eagle, and Osprey, which breed on other islands in the Green Bay National Wildlife Refuge, as well as Coyote, White-tailed Deer, Western Fox Snake, Eastern Grey Treefrog, and East-

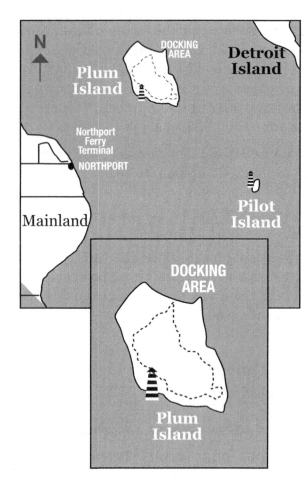

ern Spring Peeper.

Plum Island is surrounded by a rocky ledge shoreline, which varies as lake levels increase and decrease. The island is covered by Northern Mesic and Northern Wet Mesic forests dominated by Eastern White Cedar, Eastern Hemlock, Sugar Maple, and Aspen.

Take advantage of hiking at this unique spot, with a trip or workday out to the island offered by one of the charter boats from Ellison Bay or Gills Rock, the Friends of Plum and Pilot Island, the Door County Maritime Museum, or by kayaking or taking a private boat out to the island.

There are about 4.0 miles of trails on the island, but the premier trails are the Fern Island Trail, and the Eagle View Trail, which run parallel to one another a few hundred feet apart, between the old Coast Guard Station and Boathouse area and the Lightkeeper's House and Upper Rangelight. Both trails are about 0.5 miles in length, and you can take one out and the other back. If you have more time on the island, you can take the Island View Trail around the island's perimeter, which is about 3.0 miles. This trail can be inundated with water in places when lake levels are high and is subject to closures to protect rare plants and animals.

Trails, Access, & Facilities: This area has no facilities. Plum Island is open dawn to dusk in the summer months. Leashed dogs are permitted. Abide by the rules for brushing off clothing to prevent invasive species, docking boats, and general prohibited activities on the island. Bring your own food and water as no services are available on the island.

Contact: Green Bay National Wildlife Refuge, https://www.fws.gov/refuge/green_bay/. Friends of Plum and Pilot Island, www.plumandpilot.org. No fee to visit.

CHAPTER NINE

WASHINGTON ISLAND & ROCK ISLAND

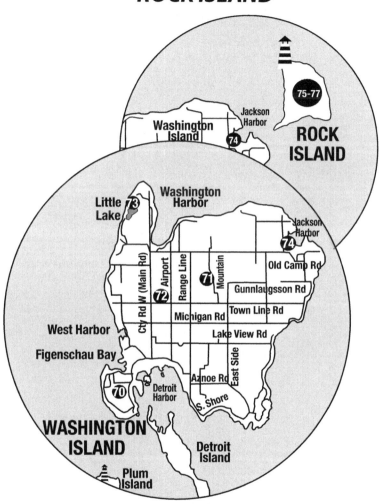

70. **Detroit Harbor State Natural Area-Richter Community Forest and Heritage Nature Trail**
71. **Mountain Park Lookout Tower**
72. **Domer-Neff Nature Preserve and Bird Sanctuary**
73. **Little lake Nature Preserve**
74. **Jackson Harbor Ridges and Carlin's Point**
75-77. **Rock Island State Park**

CHAPTER 9.

WASHINGTON ISLAND and ROCK ISLAND

Washington Island, the largest of the Grand Traverse Islands and Wisconsin's largest island, lies a short ferry ride north of the Door Peninsula. This 25-square mile island has been a classic day trip for travelers to Door County for more than a century. The best way to explore the island is by bringing a car or bike over on the Washington Island Ferry Line from Northport. Once you're on the Washington Island, you can take a second ferry, known as the Carfi, over to the smaller Rock Island, a Wisconsin State Park. At 25 square miles, Washington Island is bigger than you may think, but with only 650 permanent residents, it feels remote. The only town, if you could call it that, is the settlement at Detroit Harbor, when you arrive from the ferry.

Like much of Door County, Washington Island was first permanently settled in the mid-1800s by Icelandic, Norwegian, and Swedish farmers, loggers, and fishermen. Today, that same rural character dominates the island, with farms growing potatoes and wheat, with homes, shops, churches, a few restaurants, motels, museums, boatyards, and a 9-hole golf course. Though Washington Island hums with tourists in the summer months, the island is still a quiet place, well-suited for drives and bike trips along back roads and trips to the beach to take a dip in the cool waters of Lake Michigan on hot summer days.

Washington Island and Rock Island are only accessible by ferry or by private boat. Rock Island has no roads, and the ferry to Rock Island is passengers only.

70. Detroit Harbor State Natural Area – Richter Community Forest and Heritage Nature Trail

Detroit Harbor is the main harbor formed at the southeastern end of Washington Island. Together with Detroit Island to the south of Washington Island, this area provides critically important habitat for a diversity of plants and animals and has been designated a Wisconsin State Natural Area. The Washington Island portion of the State Natural Area is spread across a number of Door County Land Trust properties, including the Detroit Harbor Nature Preserve on Lobdell's Point Road and the Richter Community Forest, which includes 160 acres on Green Bay Road, both located to the north and west of the ferry dock

The Richter Community Forest tract is a great place for a short hike or for orchid enthusiasts and photographers seeking rare orchids in the spring and early summer. Richter Community Forest has a 1.75-mile loop trail, maintained by the Door County Land Trust, that links up with a 1.0-mile Town of Washington trail, called the Heritage Nature Trail, and dedicated to some of Washington Island's early settlers.

The trails are an easy walk for all ages. Once situated at the bottom of ancient Lake Nippising, Richter Community Forest contains ledges formed as Lake Michigan's levels dropped about 5,000 years ago as the glaciers receded. These bedrock ridges and outcrops are some of the most unique features of the property.

The area has large stands of old Eastern White Cedar trees in a Northern Wet Mesic Forest, along with sections of Northern Mesic Forest, mostly American Beech, Red Oak, Sugar Maple, and White Pine, which provides nesting habitat for Black-and-White Warbler, Cedar Waxwing, and American Redstart. In late spring and early summer, you can find a number of species of orchid, including Pink and Yellow-Lady's Slipper Orchids. Pockets of Northern Dry Mesic Forest, particularly along Lake Michigan, are primarily Red Pine and

White Pine, which provide habitat for Hoary Bat and Ermine.

You can pick up the Door County Land Trust trail from the shoulder of Green Bay Road and head north on the loop trail for about 0.8 miles until you come to the Heritage Nature Trail. You can either take the Heritage Nature Trail out to the end at Lobdell's Point Road and then retract your steps back, or you can take the loop to the right, heading back south for about 0.75-mile back to your car.

Trails: The Richter Community Forest property has about 2.5 miles of trails total, including the 1.50-mile Door County Land Trust trail and the 1.0-mile Town of Washington Heritage Nature Trail. Leashed dogs are permitted. Bikes, horses, and motorized vehicles are prohibited. Hunting is authorized in some areas pursuant to DCLT guidelines and permission.

Contact and Directions: Door County Land Trust, http://www.doorcountylandtrust.org/. Town of Washington, http://www.washingtonisland-wi.gov. The Richter Community Forest tract can be accessed from the Door

County Land Trust trailhead located across the road from 301 Green Bay Road, Washington, WI 54246. The Heritage Trail trailhead is on Lobdell Point Road, a short distance from the Washington Island Ferry landing. You can access the trail from either end.

71. Mountain Park Lookout Tower

Calling this a hike might be a bit of an overstatement, but Mountain Park Lookout Tower should be a stop on any Washington Island trip. The 184-step lookout tower is the park's primary attraction, and depending on how fast you climb, you can be at the top in a matter of a few minutes.

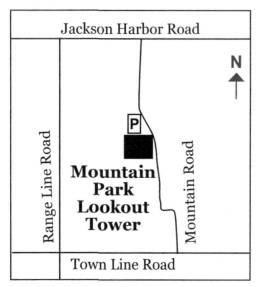

The tower sits atop Little Mountain, a ridge that forms the highest point on Washington Island. The tower features two main viewing platforms, a lower platform and the top platform, with several benches to rest and appreciate the views. In recent years the tower has become a bit worse for the wear, and there is discussion of improving it, shoring it up, or tearing it down and rebuilding it altogether.

The top provides 360-degree panoramic views the entire island, and on clear days you can see Rock Island, Detroit

Island, St. Martin Island in Michigan, and parts of Michigan's Upper Peninsula. In the spring and fall, look for migrating hawks and songbirds.

Trails, Access & Facilities: This park has no formal trails. The park has a 184-step wooden lookout tower, parking, and picnic tables.

Contact and Directions: Town of Washington, http://www.washingtonisland-wi.gov. The park entrance is at 1403 Mountain Rd., Washington, WI 54246. No fee.

72. Domer – Neff Nature Preserve and Bird Sanctuary

Forty-Three-acre Domer-Neff Nature Preserve and Bird Sanctuary features the Marilyn Domer Birding Trail, a 0.5-mile trail maintained in the summer months by the Door County Land Trust.

This 0.5-mile trail is mowed through fields and is maintained for birding and nature viewing. This trail provides good opportunities to see grassland birds, including Field Sparrow, American Kestrel, East-

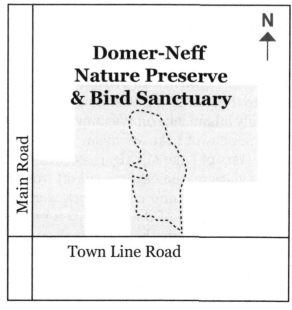

ern Kingbird, Eastern Bluebird, Clay-colored Sparrow, and Eastern Meadowlark. The trail is also an easy walk for those who have difficulty walking long distances or are walking with small children. The neighboring Stavkirke Chapel also has a meditation loop if you're interested in a longer walk and a bit of local Scandinavian culture.

Trails: There is one short 0.5-mile mowed loop path nature trail available during the summer months.

Contact: Door County Land Trust, http://www.door-countylandtrust.org/. The birding trail is on the left side of the road at 1800 Town Line Rd., Washington, WI 54246, across from Trinity Lutheran Church, 1763 Town Line Rd., just east of Main Rd. next to Stavkirke, a Norwegian Stave Church. Parking is available at either Trinity Lutheran or Stavkirke church, space permitting. Access the trail from the trailhead marked with DCLT signage on Town Line Road or from the Stavkirke prayer path marked "Birding Path." No fee.

73. Little Lake Nature Preserve

The Door County Land Trust maintains a 1.25-mile hiking trail to the shores of Little Lake, a shallow 33-acre lake and the only inland lake on Washington Island. Little Lake was a former bay of Lake Michigan 3,000-5,000 years ago. As the waters of Lake Michigan receded following the retreat of the glaciers, the bay was cut off from Lake Michigan as silt, settlement, and cobble rock were gradually deposited at the mouth of the bay. Even in wettest years, Little Lake is rarely more than six feet deep in the deepest spots, which makes it an excellent place for beginning kayakers or canoers to learn the ropes or for keen wildlife watchers to explore the shorelines by canoe or kayak or along the main hiking trail. During dry times, the lake levels drop, and the area is more of a wetland.

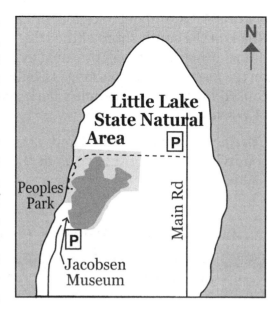

The Door County Land Trust owns a 32-acre site on the north side of the lake, which is home to pockets of deciduous Northern Wet Mesic Forest, within a large Northern Sedge Meadow wetlands and fen area. This area is home to many rare and threatened plants and animals and has been designated as a Wisconsin State Natural Area. This area is also an important Potawatomi Indian archaeological site.

In the summer look for nesting Black-throated Blue Warbler, Red-Shouldered Hawk, and breeding Blue-spotted Salamander, Little Brown Bat, and Northern Leopard Frog. In the shallows along the lakeshore, watch Great Blue Herons hunting for frogs and fish. Given its unique geography, during spring and fall migration, this spot along the edge of Washington Island can be an excellent place to look for migrant songbirds that "fall out" after flying over Lake Michigan and stop on the first available land.

Trails, Access & Facilities: The Door County Land Trust parcel can only be accessed by crossing private land via conservation easement, starting at the trailhead at 2285 Main Road, Washington, WI 54246. On this private stretch, stay on the trail and respect the private landowners along the trail. You can view the lake and the State

Natural Area, and put in canoes or kayaks from Little Lake Road on the south shore of the lake. Paddling the site requires bringing a kayak or canoe over from the mainland on the ferry. Limited parking is available at the nearby Jacobsen Museum and People's Park operated by the Town of Washington.

Contact: Door County Land Trust, http://www.doorcountylandtrust.org/.2285 Main Rd., Washington, WI 54246. No fee.

74. Jackson Harbor Ridges & Carlin's Point

In tiny, picturesque Jackson Harbor, in the northeastern corner of Washington Island, you'll find the Jackson Harbor Ridges State Natural Area. All of Washington Island is technically part of the Town of Washington, and the town operates this as a park and beach for local residents and visitors.

Jackson Harbor Ridges is a great spot for picnics or a dip in Lake Michigan, as well as a boat launch for kayak, standup paddleboard, and canoe trips out around nearby Carlin's Point, Rock Island, or Hog Island. The park features a 9-acre sandy swimming beach and two short hiking trails.

Jackson Harbor Ridges got its name from the series of twelve, low, wooded ridges and damp swales found in the park. As you might find at other Great Lakes Ridge and Swale communities in Door County, these forested ridges and wetland swales were formed by glaciers and got their shape as Lake Michigan's waters receded following the last glaciation.

Jackson Harbor Ridges is one of the few places on Door County with substantial tracts of Boreal Forest, with dense stands of White Spruce and Black Spruce, with some Northern Wet Mesic Forests of Eastern White Cedar, and some Northern Mesic Forests of Red Maple interspersed. Along the beach areas, you'll

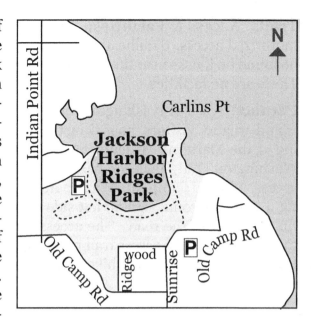

find open, upper dunes, home to several endangered and threatened plants such as Dwarf Lake Iris, Dune Thistle and Dune Goldenrod, and rare interdunal wetlands. These interdunal wetlands are damp areas between the dunes which contain a number of plants atypical of Door County, including Low Calamint, Twigrush, Bird's-eye Primrose, Baltic Rush, and Slender Bog Arrow-grass. In the summer, look for Boreal Forest birds like Blackburnian, Canada and Yellow-rumped Warblers, and Winter Wren and animals like Red Squirrel and Porcupine. This beach is also occasionally used by migrant shorebirds during spring and fall migration.

Jackson Harbor Ridges has two well maintained <1.0-mile nature trails along the shore and out to Carlin's Point. The main Jackson Harbor Ridges Trail meanders along the harbor for about 0.5 miles and provides lake views and views of Hog Island, part of the Green Bay National Wildlife Refuge. The Carlin's Point Trail, a 0.3-mile trail, provides views of Rock Island State Park's historic boathouse, just offshore.

Trails, Access & Facilities: Trails are limited to non-motorized access. Trailheads and detailed trail maps can be found on kiosks near the Jackson Harbor Ridges beach. There are no facilities.

Contact: Town of Washington, http://www.washington-island-wi.gov. Visitors can pick up the trails by either parking at the Maritime Museum, 1902 Jackson Harbor Rd., Washington, WI 54246, or parking at the Carlin's Point access, 280 Old Camp Rd., Washington, WI 54246. Watch for a 'Carlin's Point' sign on left side of the road. Park off the shoulder of the road. The access trail is 0.1-miles to the point where the access trail meets the Jackson Harbor Ridges Trail. Turn right to hike to the end of Carlin's Point (a 0.4-mile trail). No fee.

75. Rock Island State Park—Thordarson Loop

Rock Island is Wisconsin's most difficult to access state park. It is not a place for anyone to find themselves in by accident—getting here requires not one, but two, ferry rides. You won't find any tourist facilities, restaurants, hotels, or cars on the island, just a gorgeous turn of the century traditional Icelandic-style boathouse, the state park's campground, which maintains a small concessionaire staffed by a summer naturalist, a water tower, historic Potawatomi Lighthouse, and the ruins of a few historic buildings. While you can get water and snacks at the campground, you'll need to bring provisions over from Washington Island.

However, the novelty of the journey and the scenic beauty of the park makes the difficulty in getting here worthwhile in the end. This is an especially memorable spot for a family overnight camping trip. If you've come for an overnight trip, you'll want to take on the Thordarson Loop Trail, a 5.2-mile roundtrip trail around the entire perimeter of Rock Island. The trail passes all of the hotspots on the

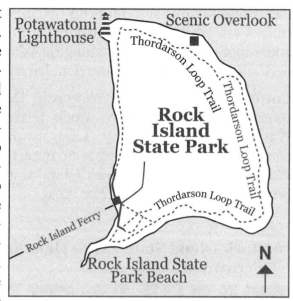

island listed above, including the Potawatomi Lighthouse, one of the oldest lighthouses on the Great Lakes, which dates to 1836.

The trail is named after the Thordarson family, who originally settled on Rock Island in the early 1900s. More than 60 years later, the family sold the entire island to the State of Wisconsin, creating the state's first and only island state park. This trail is incredibly straightforward and offers essentially uninterrupted obscured views of Lake Michigan through the trees throughout the entire 5.2-mile loop. A summer walk around the island will reveal breeding birds like Northern Parula, Black-throated Green Warbler, Canada Warbler, Blackburnian Warbler, and American Redstart.

Trails, Access & Facilities: Rock Island State Park is technically open year-round, but the Carfi ferry only runs seasonally, generally from Memorial Day to Labor Day. The trails are generally flat, easy to moderate hiking. No bicycles or motorized vehicles are allowed. Camping areas are located in the southwestern portion of the island and must be reserved in advance through the Wisconsin State

Parks reservations system. Primitive facilities, water, and snacks are available, but you must bring your own food and supplies over from Washington Island. Check at the park's Visitor Center for more detailed trail information.

Contact & Directions: Wisconsin Dept. Natural Resources, http://dnr.wi.gov. Rock Island Ferry (Carfi), Washington Island Ferry Line, http://www.wisferry.com/. Parking for the Carfi is at 1924 Indian Point Rd., Washington, WI 54246. Rock Island is also accessible by private boat. Fee for ferry. Fee area.

76. Rock Island State Park—Hauamai and Fernwood Trails

Located just northeast from Washington Island, 999-acre Rock Island State Park is accessible by the passenger-only "Carfi" ferry from Jackson Harbor on Washington Island. There are many daily ferry sailings during the summer season, so you can visit Rock Island as a day trip or plan to camp overnight (reserve well in advance). In the fall and winter, Rock Island can be accessed only by private boat or by snowmobile in years when the Jackson Harbor stretch to Washington Island freezes solid.

Rock Island has more than ten miles of trails, including two less traveled trails—the Fernwood Trail, 1.2 miles, and the Hauamal Trail, 1.1 miles, which run across the middle and southern 1/3 of the island respectively, and both link up with the Thordarson Loop Trail at either end.

From the ferry landing, you can take the Thordarson Trail down and pick up either Hauamal or Fernwood Trails and then take the other trail on the way back for a roundtrip hike of a little more than 3.5 miles. If you're looking for a slightly less traveled route, particularly on summer weekends, these trails are a great choice.

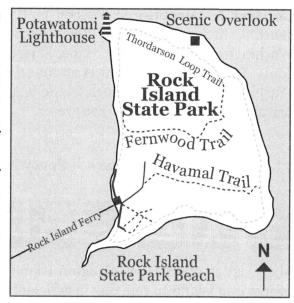

The Fernwood and Hauamal Trails will take you through the middle of the island— the portion of the island that is designated as a State Natural Area. You'll walk through majestic groves of White Spruce, Red Maple, Eastern White Cedar, and American Beech forests and rocky outcrops on the interior of the island. Moist Cliff communities, associated with these rocky outcrops, host a number of fern species and Large-flowered Trillium and provide habitat for Northern Ring-necked Snake and ground-nesting birds like Ovenbird and Mourning Warbler. This is the quieter and less trafficked part of the park on summer weekends, and you will have the place to yourself in the off season.

Trails, Access & Facilities: Rock Island State Park is open year round, but the Carfi ferry only runs seasonally, generally from Memorial Day to Labor Day. The trails are generally flat, easy to moderate hiking. No bicycles or motorized vehicles are allowed. Camping areas are located in the southwestern portion of the island and must be reserved in advance through the Wisconsin State Parks reservations system. Primitive facilities, water, and snacks are available, but you must bring your own food and supplies over from Washington Island. Check at the park's Visitor Center for more detailed trail information.

Contact & Directions: Wisconsin Dept. Natural Resources, http://dnr.wi.gov. Rock Island Ferry (Carfi), Washington Island Ferry Line, http://www.wisferry.com/. Parking for the Carfi is at 1924 Indian Point Rd., Washington, WI 54246. Rock Island is also accessible by private boat. Fee for ferry. Fee area.

77. Rock Island State Park – Ferry Landing to Lighthouse Route

Many day-trippers to Washington Island find the novelty of just one island in one day insufficient. A second ferry ride, out to Rock Island, part of the Wisconsin State Parks System, via the "Carfi", may be just the thing to complete your Door County experience.

The Carfi to Rock Island State Park runs from May to October, and the island offers camping, swimming, hiking, and kayaking. A visit to the island's historic 1836-era light-

house is the classic Rock Island hike, especially if you only have a few hours between Carfi pick up and drop off.

The 2.5-mile roundtrip trail along a portion of the Thordarson Loop between the ferry landing and the Potowatomi Lighthouse is the most popular hike on the island, and the campground and lighthouse areas can be busy on summer weekends. Visit mid-week or during the off-season if you want to get that private island feeling.

Following the trip to the lighthouse, if you find yourself with extra time on your hands, you can enjoy the beach and boathouse area adjacent to the campground, which boasts a large Cliff Swallow colony, and

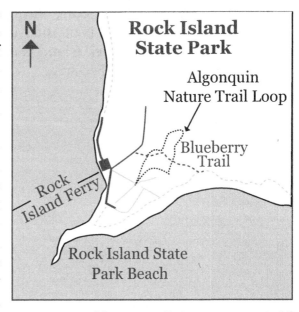

drifting Caspian Terns, Double-crested Cormorant, Bald Eagle, Osprey, and Ring-billed Gulls can be seen flying past the docks in the summer months. The Algonquin Nature Trail Loop and the Blueberry Trails are in the area of the beach and offer short hikes. In the fall, Rock Island can be an exceptional place to watch fall songbird and raptor migration.

Trails, Access & Facilities: Rock Island State Park is open year round, but the Carfi ferry only runs seasonally, generally from Memorial Day to Labor Day. The trails are generally flat, easy to moderate hiking. No bicycles or motorized vehicles are allowed. Camping areas are located in the southwestern portion of the island and must be reserved in advance through the Wisconsin State Parks reservations system. Primitive facilities, water, and snacks are available, but you must bring your own food and supplies over from Washington Island. Check at the park's Visitor Center for more detailed trail information.

Contact & Directions: Wisconsin Dept. Natural Resources, http://dnr.wi.gov. Rock Island Ferry (Carfi), Washington Island Ferry Line, http://www.wisferry.com/. Parking for the Carfi is at 1924 Indian Point Rd., Washington, WI 54246. Rock Island is also accessible by private boat. Fee for ferry. Fee area.

Made in the USA
Middletown, DE
04 June 2022

66604823R00116